Conversations
with a
dancer

*Conversations
with a
dancer*

A Dance Horizons Book

Kitty Cunningham with Michael Ballard

St. Martin's Press, New York

I would like to acknowledge the enthusiasm of Al Pischl, the advice of Selma Jeanne Cohen, the editorial help of Mary D. Kierstead, and for a combination of all three, Francis Cunningham.

Library of Congress Cataloging in Publication Data

Cunningham, Kitty.
Conversations with a dancer.

1. Ballard, Michael.   2. Dancers—United
States—Biography.   I. Title.
GV1785.B343C86   793.3'2'0924 [B] 80–14266
ISBN 0–312–16942–6

A portion of this book first appeared in *Dance Magazine*. It is reproduced with the kind permission of Danad Publishing Company, Inc.

All photos in the text were taken by Norman Ader, with the exception of the photo of Michael Ballard and Anne McLeod on p. 150, which was taken by John A. VanLund.

This book is dedicated to
the Murray Louis Dance Company

MURRAY LOUIS

JANIS BRENNER

RICHARD HAISMA

WILLIAM HOLAHAN

HELEN KENT

DIANNE MARKAM

ANNE MCLEOD

JERRY PEARSON

SARA PEARSON

DANIAL SHAPIRO

ROBERT SMALL

MARCIA WARDELL

Photos by: TOM CARAVAGLIA

Author's Note

The works by Murray Louis mentioned in the text and listed in the appendix form only a part of Louis's choreographic opus. Since 1953 Murray Louis has created more than seventy dances. Most of these works have been performed by his own company, although he has worked with ballet companies in Germany (1974), Scotland (1975), and Denmark (1975, 1976), and in addition has choreographed for Rudolf Nureyev.

Throughout his professional life Murray Louis has been closely associated with Alwin Nikolais, first as his student, then as a teacher at the Henry Street Playhouse and as an outstanding dancer in the Nikolais company, and as co-director of the Nikolais/Louis Foundation for Dance, the present school and home for both the Louis and Nikolais dance companies. The association between Louis and Nikolais is one of the closest and most lasting in the creative arts field. Most dancers eventually break with their mentors; Louis and Nikolais still work together, although their companies remain separate and completely distinguishable.

Whereas Nikolais blends movement into other stage elements so that the dancers are no more than equal to the costumes, lighting, and sets, in Louis's works it is always the dancer who is foremost; his works emphasize the bite and wit of unexpected movement and the electric energy which charges out of the performers. It is this energy that most characterizes Louis as a dancer and choreographer.

Contents

Foreword

Michael Ballard is familiar to the dance world, having been a member of the Murray Louis Dance Company for the past seven years. He grew up in Denver, Colorado, and graduated from the University of Utah in 1965 with a degree in dance. He has appeared nationally and internationally both on the concert stage and on television with the Louis company and is currently soloist and dance captain. The title role of Scheherazade *was choreographed especially for him. He has in addition appeared with the Nikolais company for several years during their extensive tours nationally and abroad.*

Program note from the Murray Louis Dance Company, 1976.

This book of conversations with a dancer started for the sheer fun of talking about dance. How does dance happen? What are the considerations before, during, and after a performance? What is it like, being in a modern dance company today? Who *is* the dancer of today? What lies behind the brief biography listed in a dance program?

As a writer on dance I had wondered about the training, the discipline, and the compulsion which brings someone to the stage. There are few records of the dancer's daily life, of the growth of a performing artist, and of the business of working for a choreographer in a major dance company. Michael Ballard always answered all my questions, drawing on his ten years' experience of professional dancing, first with Alwin Nikolais and then with Murray Louis.

We began talking about how Michael became a dancer. Then, because we were enjoying ourselves, we continued talking, discussing the care and feeding of a dancer, touring, the body, the teaching and choreography of Alwin Nikolais and Murray Louis, being a dancer in America today, performing, and watching others perform. We covered everything I had wondered about concerning dance and touched on many things that I had not even started to consider.

Our conversations began in a motel room in Moscow, Idaho, in March, 1975 and they continued wherever and whenever we could get a chance to talk: in the Berkshire Hills in Massachusetts; a cemetery in Saratoga Springs; a psychiatrist's office in New York (the only quiet place I could find); a hotel in Philadelphia; and, in Buenos Aires, Argentina. In 1975–76 the Murray Louis Dance Company toured more than any other modern dance company, and sometimes I traveled with them.

This is a book about performing, and about the work and pleasure that one dancer has experienced in his chosen profession. In one of our talks Michael said: "On the stage, just the fact of the people out there demands a whole other kind of existence from you. You don't go out there and live your life. You go out there and the energy has to come out, because if it doesn't, you don't belong there. That's what a stage is. It's a dancing ground, a place where larger things happen. It's a magic place. Miss Ruth [St. Denis] and Martha [Graham] gave the stage divine connotations. That's probably what man's sense of divinity and spirituality is—a thing larger than himself. Every performer who is a real performer has that and knows how to work it, how to expand it, and then, after the performance, how to let go and come back to earth, so to speak."

What follows is a description of how performing—the other kind of existence—takes place.

Kitty Cunningham

Preface

April 1976

FERNWOOD COMMUNITY COLLEGE

in cooperation with
the Ohio Council on the Arts
and the National Endowment for the Arts

presents

THE MURRAY LOUIS DANCE COMPANY

choreography by MURRAY LOUIS

Performed by MURRAY LOUIS, MICHAEL BALLARD, *Richard Haisma, Helen Kent,*
Anne McLeod, Dianne Markham, Jerry Pearson, Sara Pearson, Robert Small

It is eight o'clock on a Friday night. People are hurrying down the aisles of the college auditorium, anxious to be seated before the lights go down. There is a pleasant buzz of conversation from the crowd—three-quarters students, faculty, and staff, the rest from the surrounding community, all gathered to share in an evening of theater. Many are animated, expectant; some are pensive; still others are resentful at having this forced upon them by their spouses or offspring. There is much calling out and waving to neighbors.

Behind the curtain the bare stage is dimly lit and the atmosphere is made dense by the steady hum from the auditorium. The dancers, wearing sweat clothes over their costumes, in exaggerated makeup, are quietly performing last-minute rituals for warming and limbering their bodies. There is not much conversation; this is a moment of reflection before a massive outpouring of energy, involving the concentrated effort of body, mind, and psyche.

Murray Louis himself is pacing backstage, restless, joking with the crew, wanting the performance to begin. He appears only in the second piece of the evening, his brilliant solo *Chimera*. He's told there will be a seven-minute hold because there's a line at the box office; this visibly increases his restlessness. All the dancers are unhappy with the news—they have consciously or unconsciously pitched themselves to begin, and holding back now is torturous.

A certain delicacy of mood is broken. Helen [Kent] remembers that she needs to be pinned in, and Anne [McLeod] goes to her aid, pinning her bra strap inside her costume. Richard [Haisma] dashes off to the dressing room to get a towel he forgot, returning moments later and leaving it in the wings. The time seems long.

Tony Miccoci, the stage manager, finally announces, "Places," and everyone sheds practice clothes to reveal the simple, beautiful white costumes for *Porcelain Dialogues*. Each dancer sits on a tape mark, together forming a semicircle opening out to the audience. But the dancers are facing away from center stage. What was a moment ago a neutral space has suddenly been colored by the placement and attitude of six performers.

I, one of the dancers, am fairly calm because this is a regularly performed ballet in our repertory. Yet, as I hear the audience bustle subside (house lights are dimming), and the stage goes dark, I feel a small clutching deep inside. What I am doing here with my fellows is important, is significant on an intimate scale, as a communal event, with aesthetics as its ground and its reason for being. For all my warm-up, my hands and feet are clammy; there is a strong expectant vibration coming from the audience. My responsibility to them is great, and I feel it every time. The curtains part, the lights dim, the music begins. I turn around on cue, as do all my partners. I am exposed—we are naked before the curiosity and anticipation. The moment is supercharged; the event, the communion, has already begun.

If someone asked me, why are you a dancer, I would have to say that my joy is to communicate on an aesthetic level with my fellow human beings. I have gravitated to that which is most natural to me

—dancing. In Murray Louis's choreography and direction I find physical, mental, and psychic release, and I am grateful that my life has led me on this fabulously rewarding path.

This book explains, I think, some of the richness to be mined in the art of performing. To someone from my prosaic, middle-class, midwestern background, such a career is exotic and undreamed-of, and I feel lucky beyond counting to have arrived where I am, simply because the opportunities for the soul's expansion are so varied and so insistent.

Michael Ballard

Falling
into
dance

*Background: Colorado; Utah; New York
with Alwin Nikolais and Murray Louis
—dancing, learning, teaching.*

Our first conversation took place in Moscow, Idaho
—Dry Pea and Lentil Capital of the World and
home of the University of Idaho. It was Easter
Sunday. After a company day off, Michael and I had
a nightcap in my motel room at the Royal Motor
Inn.

What is a nice boy like you doing in a town like this? How did you
get here?

I'm here because I love to dance, I love to move, and I love to be on
stage in front of people. The moving part is strange because before I
was a dancer I didn't like to move at all. I wasn't interested in sports.
I must say I rode my bicycle back and forth from school, but that was
the only physical thing I did. In grade school at recess time I just sat
around and watched everybody else but maybe that's because I was
very shy and didn't take to group activities very well. But then falling
into dance, and I really did fall because it was almost by accident . . .
I took my first dance course, which was an excuse to get out of a
physical education requirement as a freshman at the University of
Colorado back in 1960–61.

I didn't know I was going to like dance so much, I had no idea.
I was taking a ballroom dance course, as a matter of fact, and I asked
my instructor who happened to be the modern dance teacher at
Colorado, "What is modern dance?" And she said, "Well, it's sort of

a combination of ballet and gymnastics." And so I said, "Well, all right, I'll try it out."

And so I did the whole thing. The day before I had to go up to my first class I phoned the instructor and said, "Do I need any special clothes or equipment to take this class?" And she said, "You need a dance belt and a pair of tights and maybe a T-shirt because we like to see what your body is doing." So I went down to Colorado Costumes in Denver and got a pair of these god-awful cotton tights—wrestler's tights I think they were, black with feet in—and a dance belt, which was an article of apparel I had no experience with.

I showed up for class the next day and a bunch of us students were waiting in the hall and there I was in my cotton tights with the feet in and one of the girls said to me (this was in the women's gym) "Gee, I didn't know this was a coed class." And that made me feel "real positive" about it right away, of course.

During the first class they said I would have to cut the feet out of my tights and so on. But then the capper came at the end of the class when the teacher came up to me and said, "You've had modern dance before, haven't you?" and I said "No I've never moved at all in my life. This is completely new to me." And she said "Oh, well." And immediately there's an interest, because any time a boy can move they get interested.

Were you the only one in the class?

I was the only boy in the class, right. It was a very basic beginning modern dance class which most of the girls were taking because it was part of their physical education requirement.

When you had to get out of Phys. Ed., how did you discover you could take dance?

Dance was one of the alternatives. I had my choice between volleyball and dance. So I chose dance because I'm deathly afraid of balls coming at me. I just cringe rather than hit them or catch them or whatever you have to do to them. One time when I was a cub scout, we were forced out on the field to play softball and I was out in center field hoping that no one would notice me and a ball came toward me and I put out my hands to catch it. It jammed my thumb and it hurt so badly that I didn't know what to do. So I stuck out the game with nary a quiver of the lip but when I got home I screamed.

I stomped upstairs and said, "I'll never play softball again as long as I live." And I haven't. That was my sports career. In toto.

But you did take more dance classes?

Yes. Now the first one was in the final quarter of my freshman year in the spring—the end of the school year—but I intended to stay on for summer school at Colorado and Merce Cunningham was giving a three-week workshop that summer. So I said to my teacher, "Do you think I'm ready or good enough to take the Cunningham workshop?" And she said, "No, but take it anyway." And so I did. Madness. Well, summer time is very pleasant in Boulder, so I could go around with bare feet all the time and I did, because in the Cunningham workshop I did such strenuous things with my feet that I got blisters on the bottoms of my feet which were very tender of course, because I'd always worn shoes. And so in order to toughen up my feet I went to every class, I went everywhere, in my bare feet. My speech teacher was very amused, but I stood up in front of her class and gave my speeches in bare feet. At that time Colorado was known as a play school, especially during the summer sessions. Going barefoot was perfectly all right because everyone expected a little avant garde, fun attitude.

How was the Cunningham workshop?

Oh I was terribly stimulated by it all. I found that the more I did the more my appetite increased for it so I threw myself into it. It was a very exciting time. It was the best time of my life I think, the first two years of college. I was away from home, on my own, discovering all kinds of things on my own, being out from under at home. And then this dance thing came along. I was casting around for something to do with my life, and suddenly something came and it just *took* me and I was swept along. It wasn't my will. I did it because I had to.

During my second year at Colorado I technically majored in theater. I had no idea of dancing as a career then. So I majored in theater but I kept on dancing. I was in a couple of plays and so on, but at the end of my second year I knew I wanted to dance for a career. I had met and had had at least one class with two of the instructors from the University of Utah—Shirley Ririe and Joan Woodbury. That same summer as the Cunningham course Shirley Ririe had given a three-week course after him, so I worked with her.

Then Joan Woodbury had given a one-day seminar at one of the nearby colleges, and a bunch of us had gone up and taken it and she was wonderful, just wonderful. And so I decided to go to Utah. During the summer I broke the news to my parents and said, "I want to major in dance and I want to go to the University of Utah." There was this long silence. But my father particularly was very understanding because he always wanted me to do what I wanted to do.

The very first year I was there Nikolais and Murray were setting *Totem* on the student dancers, and I arrived too late. They were working during part of the summer and into the fall, and I arrived too late to be in *Totem*. But I worked backstage on the light board for Nikolais, and that was some experience! I saw the rehearsals and worked with everybody. It was fascinating, and I met Murray and Nik and got to know them quite well. They took a shine to me for some reason.

Then that year I worked with Joan and Shirley and Dr. Elizabeth Hayes, who was head of the department there, and in the spring, for the Spring Concert, we did a suite of the dances from *Totem*. We reconstructed them and I danced in that, and that was my first taste of dancing in Nikolais pieces to an electronic score. Big excitement. We performed in a new theater on the Utah campus. It was a theatrical event, and that of course confirmed me in what I wanted to do.

I spent three years at Utah after my two years at Colorado and I kept learning and learning and avidly eating up whatever I could get about dancing. During my last year at Utah I was taking an hour and a half ballet class and an hour and a half modern class, and with all the rehearsals we were constantly busy. Salt Lake has quite a large dance audience because Virginia Tanner, who is a fine children's dance teacher, worked there and the graduates from the University go out into the high schools there and all the high schools have dance too. So everyone's very interested. We found ourselves being invited around to various functions to give miniperformances. It was almost like a repertory of student's works that were being performed around the city. Also in my last year we had Senior Recital, in which I had to choreograph a piece and be in other people's pieces, and the Spring Concert which was a big occasion. And also in that period I had to give my own Senior Recital, my own personal recital, because I

as one of the first two students to graduate under the Bachelor of
ine Arts degree—Carolyn Carlson was the other one. We each had
) give our own personal recital of works of our own or works that we
ere in and so I was terribly busy that year, terribly busy. Anna
okolow came that year and we did two of her pieces on the Spring
oncert, the big concert. Plus Joan and Shirley collaborated on a big
rty-five minute piece in which I had the central role, and so that
as a lot of work and I was terribly overworked and underfed.

But still my intuition kept urging me on. At one point during my
me at Utah I was vacillating between becoming a ballet major or
aying a modern major and I listened to my good sense and it said,
Stick with the modern, it will serve you well." At the time I loved
y ballet classes. I loved doing that kind of movement. But my inner
ice told me to stay with the modern and I did.

After my last year at Utah I took the summer course that
ikolais gave at Utah. He said, "Come to New York and study with
e," and so I did. I had a slight interim at home while I made some
oney so I could go to New York. I nearly went crazy staying at
ome. Boy, that was an awful period. But then I went to New York
January of '66. I arrived in a snowstorm—a blizzard—and I went
the Henry Street Playhouse where Nikolais was teaching. Almost
ree weeks later Nikolais said, "I want you to join the company." I
as to be in *Vaudeville of the Elements,* which had been premiered
e fall before at the Guthrie Theater in Minneapolis, but he was
ing to revive it in the spring.

That particular year marked a milestone in the Nikolais company
cause it was the first time the company had been paid for
hearsals. Up to that time the company had taught or had jobs and
hearsed in the evening. And now for some reason there was money
r rehearsal pay. So somehow I existed. I made twenty-five dollars a
eek.

his was 1966 and you lived on twenty-five dollars a week?

ell, I scraped through that season and then came summer and there
as no work and I became a busboy at Serendipity 3 uptown and had
ite a lovely time there because of the congenial working conditions.
nd I didn't dance all that summer. I let myself get out of shape.

hy did you?

I was stupid. The job at Serendipity took a lot of energy and I had l« summers go by before without moving. So I did it, and the fall came and, boy, I remember the pain. The first class of the fall season was not bad, but the second class was so painful I thought I was going tc die. Bill Frank was my teacher for that class. I still remember the awful pain of it. But then Nikolais revived *Imago* and he started touring fairly solidly and that was about the time the government started getting interested in subsidizing the touring of the companies so we worked fairly steadily. I remember the next summer I also worked at Serendipity. I graduated to waiter. Big deal. But that was very good.

Did you take classes that summer?

In August Murray had a residence at Southampton College of Long Island University, and so for the month of August we were employec and dancing. We stayed out in Southampton in the dormitories ther· and Murray choreographed *Go 6.*

But you weren't in Murray's company?

At that time Murray and Nikolais were using all the same dancers. Murray used fewer than Nikolais but most of Murray's dancers were in Nik's company. Murray had what he called his five blonds: Phyllis Lamhut, Carolyn Carlson, Jan Strader, Wanda Pruska, and Batya Zamir. We all lived in the dormitories there and Phyllis Lamhut wa: there with her dog and it was all very chummy. *Go 6* was choreographed on the very strange stage they have there, which was very wide and very shallow. To this day *Go 6* has had problems because of the shape of that original stage. That was in '67, and it sort of eased me into the fall season.

And you were paid for that month?

Yes. Also we got dorm food, which was cheap. Anyway, there was more touring fall and spring, and that fall Nikolais choreographed *Somniloquy* and we premiered that in the Guggenheim Museum in their awful little auditorium there. But it was a smash—a smash beyond anybody's dreams. It was Nikolais's first slide piece—the first time he used slides and of course he was terribly excited about that. He choreographed *Triptych* that winter, and we did *Somniloquy* and *Triptych* as a full evening work, alternating with *Imago.*

I saw Triptych *and* Somniloquy *at the Henry Street Playhouse. It was the first Nikolais I ever saw.*

As I understand it, it was quite an astounding evening.

It was.

We went out on tour with *Imago* which had been designed to tour. It had the props folded up into little cases that could be carried, rather than great big things like *Vaudeville of the Elements,* which had long sticks and barrel-shaped things that did not fold down because it had not been designed to travel.

Our New York season was in December 1967, then we went to Hollywood on our big three-week tour. Nikolais had been to Spoleto before, but most of us in the company had never been out on tour. For three weeks we stayed at the Hollywood Knickerbocker Hotel. Then came the residence at the University of South Florida in Tampa, when Nikolais choreographed *Tent.* Joan Woodbury was also there, teaching and observing rehearsals. We were all trying to get suntans during the breaks of rehearsals, and Nikolais would get furious because we'd come back and be very logy on stage. We were torn between suntan and dedication, but evidently the dedication won out, because *Tent* came out an absolute masterpiece.

That was June of '68, and the fall after that we toured again, and then came the first European tour late in the fall of '68. We went to Sweden, Germany, Italy, Switzerland. That was a six-week tour, and I got very depressed because it was the first time I'd been to Europe and the inundation of new things and the lack of familiarity with my surroundings were terribly depressing to me. Also I overspent myself, and for a while I was without money, and it was ghastly. But still it was fascinating. We played Rome too, and I got to see the Vatican Museum, the Colosseum, and other things, which made it all worthwhile.

All during '68, rumors were running rampant that Murray and Nik were going to split companies and that Murray was going to form his own company.

Wait. During this time that you were all with Nikolais, Murray was doing what?

He was dancing with Nikolais. He had his own season at the

Playhouse. In December of '66, the first full year I was there, I danced in Murray's *Calligraph for Martyrs* when we had a season at the Playhouse, but that and *Go 6* were the only things of Murray's I was in. Then in December of 1968, Nik and Murray divided up the dancers—you take one and I take one and you take one and I take one.

Did you have any say in this?

I think our preferences were known. Murray knew what he wanted in his dancers and so he chose very carefully. Out of Nik's company he took Phyllis Lamhut and Sara Shelton (who'd only been in the company a short time, maybe a year) and myself. Out of the school he got Fran Tabor and Raymond Johnson, who'd been there for some time. Raymond had been dancing in Nikolais's company too, I guess. Raymond had been off and on because he was going to school trying to get his degree. Murray, Raymond, and me, and Fran Tabor, Sara Shelton, and Phyllis—three men and three women.

In December of '68, Murray choreographed *Proximities* and *Intersection* and a Bach solo for himself [*Concerto*], which I don't remember at all and he doesn't either. In January 1969 we had our season at the Playhouse, the first season of the new Murray Louis Dance Company. We did *Proximities* and *Intersection* and *Interims* (I learned Roger Rowell's part) and we did *Junk Dances.* Murray did his Bach solo and an earlier version of *Chimera,* which at that time I believe was still called *Charade.*

But by then it was just the Murray Louis Dance Company?

Basically it was the new company, yes. The old company—the five blonds—did *Junk Dances* the first week and we did *Junk Dances* the third week, and so we made the transfer. Probably we did *Landscapes* too. I can't remember. After that spring, Murray had a tour which I don't remember very much of, except that it was short. Then Nikolais still wanted his old company for a summer European tour, so we rehearsed for that, and in the summer of '69 we went to Europe for eight weeks and alternated *Imago* with *Tent, Tower,* and *Somniloquy.*

Anyway, we went on and on and got better and better, and the company changed. In the summer of '72 when we played at the Washington Monument it was Robert Small's first time with us. After the performance Nikolais started to rave about the company. He said,

"Murray, that is the most beautiful company in the world. I can't get over how beautiful they are." This from Alwin Nikolais, who if you were lucky said, "Good show, kid." I couldn't believe my ears because I had never heard Nikolais talk that way. Since then there have been other opinions put out by Nikolais at certain points. He keeps us in line when we start to pat ourselves on the back. Which is a good thing—Murray indulges us so much.

But Murray gets what he wants.

Yes, but Murray is a passionate person, and sometimes his passion gets in the way of his cool, aesthetic sense. And there is a danger of getting too slick and too pretty, of putting too much accent on personalities dancing rather than on the work that's being seen.

Talk about some of the differences in dancing in the two companies. When you dance in Nikolais's work can you feel what they are about?

No, you have no idea, particularly in the works which use slide projections, because the slides create the thing around you. I danced in *Tent* for two years, then I was away for a year and a half before I saw it. When I saw it I could not believe what I was seeing. I had no idea of the resonances, of the depths, of the things that clang through your mind as you're watching it. We're like engines on the stage generating an energy, the directed energy that Nikolais has taken out of us. You have no idea of the picture that's presented. It was always too bad, being in Nikolais's pieces, because everyone would come back and say, "Mindblowing," and you'd say, "Oh really? Pardon me while I go pack my case."

Dancers go through the training and become dancers, I feel, because they have an exhibitionistic tendency, because they want to be seen. Maybe they were neglected in their childhood or whatever, I don't know, but they want to be up there and they want people to see them and they want people to know what they are doing.

If, as in the Nikolais company, they are shrouded on the stage and covered up, they get to feeling as if they are not fulfilling what they want to do. That's an understandable emotional reaction. So the dedication to Nikolais the man and Nikolais the artist has to pull you through. I feel my power as a performer was given great impetus by dancing in Murray's pieces, whereas in Nikolais's pieces I really always felt like the background, although I learned a great deal. Of course I was not as skilled a performer then as I am now.

Dancing for Murray is wonderful. I share a great deal of his romantic temperament. He opens himself to his feelings very strongly in his choreography, and that appeals to me because it's not cerebral at all. Everything he choreographs is sincerely felt—if at first only in the muscles, later on it works into the deeper recesses of the mind and the emotions. That's marvelously fulfilling to me. There's nothing like it.

Murray does dancy dances which, if you want to be very crude about it, consist of steps done to music with a beat. That's what dancy dancing is. Nikolais's work consists of having to be very sensitive psychically, improvisationally, to the environment and the impulses of the other dancers, and at the same time to be participating in whatever is going on on the stage. As directed by Nikolais. Nikolais would give you a chunk of time in which he wanted a certain thing to happen and you were free to improvise within a certain structure to attain that end. When that chunk of time ended you heard a music cue and you went on to the next span of time. Then another thing would be happening. You would have, say, twenty seconds to get from this part of the stage to that part of the stage executing a certain kind of movement, but what you did within that was rather free.

Murray, on the other hand, shows you with his body what he wants and you learn that step. Then you do it and he watches it and makes suggestions about how to do it or not to do it, or an overall dynamic approach or musical approach to what is done.

So the difference is that in Murray's pieces you have a sense of very strong movement structure; Nikolais's pieces feel more open. To the typical dancer it is more satisfying to do Murray's things because you have a sense of actually accomplishing something. In Nikolais's work you are subject to everything that is going on around you and you are only the fifth part of what was coming out to the audience, whereas in Murray's things you have the feeling that you are in control and that *you* are giving to the audience what they're getting. I think maybe that's the basic difference as a performer. As I told you, when I saw Nikolais's things later on I had tears in my eyes because I had no idea how beautiful they were. A performer, I think, can get easily frustrated if he doesn't realize what's coming across. He

esn't feel in control. He feels almost the subject, or the acted upon
ther than the actor.

Tent, *the tent is the subject.*

Tent, of course, the star is the tent. And you feel it very much on
age, that thing is so gorgeous.

*it it wouldn't be anything if it weren't for the human beings. It has
be ten human beings doing the right thing.*

ght. Doing the correct thing. I think I read somewhere that
ikolais said he uses his dancers as generators, and that's a very apt
scription of what a dancer is in Nikolais's pieces. But I wanted to
more. I wanted to be in control of what was going on, and I very
uch get that sense in Murray's pieces.

And when Murray uses classical music there's no greater joy for
e. Like dancing to Brahms or dancing to Tchaikovsky. Or the *Bach
ite* that we're reviving now. It's the joy of living, and to be on the
age doing it for other people is the other half of it.

heherazade *is something even more, I think.*

course my role, Scheherazade, is a whole narrative within itself.
ie first part of the second act, the first glimpse you have of
heherazade surrounded by the others in what we call the rainbow
nce, which is done to the first movement, is a stunning dance. That
s the first thing that was choreographed way back in its first draft.
eel sinful when I dance it because I enjoy it too much. I know that
houldn't be feeling what I'm feeling when I'm dancing that.
iere's one section in it where my stomach muscles are used in a
id of contracting-releasing way. This is in a group section so you
n't see me particularly doing it, because everyone is doing it. Your
iotional center is down there in the solar plexus and when you're
ing your muscles contracting and releasing very strongly in this area
u get an emotional feedback which is too strong for a performer to
having on stage and be in full control. I know that I shouldn't
joy that so much, but I take advantage of the fact that it is a group
tion and I'm not totally exposed when I do it.

The rest of the time in *Scheherazade* I'm pretty cool about my
n approach to what is going on. Except when I'm on the stool in

the second act. I'm scared to death because the lights are in my eyes
and I'm off the floor and again I'm not in full control of what's going
on. I can fall any time. It's scary. And I wonder—for the audience—
how much is the music and how much is the dance? I know the
dance is beautiful but the music is so lush and evocative too.

*The music is so familiar that it does bring up memories. The first time
I saw Murray's* Scheherazade *I remembered Yvonne DeCarlo in a
movie called* Song of Scheherazade. *You didn't conjure up Yvonne
DeCarlo; the music did. It was one of the first pieces of classical music
I ever knew. But now* Scheherazade *is that dance. It's not Yvonne
DeCarlo or my first piece of classical music. Yet in people's minds it's
not fashionable to like that kind of music. It's a very risky piece of
music to use.*

We were trembling when he finally decided to use it because we
knew the danger of the familiarity of the music. That was the first
time Murray had allowed himself to give in to his Russian passion and
he was very tentative about using that music. He said, "If it doesn't
work I'll have a score written to the dance," so we showed it to
Nikolais and Nikolais said, "That'll be a great piece when you get a
score for it." And Murray said, "You hear that, dolls?" and we said,
"Yes, we hear that." But fortunately, passion won out—and maybe
the dance finally proved itself too, as being able to overcome the
music.

You could not dance it to any other music.

Well, you could, but it wouldn't be the same. When we did the
Tchaikovsky [*Porcelain Dialogues*] Murray had an electronic score
written for it, done to the dance structured on the Tchaikovsky, and
it was ghastly. *Scheherazade* had proved to him that he could trust
his passion, and so he had no qualms about using the Tchaikovsky
until I think Nikolais convinced him that he had to have another
score written for it. So he did, and when it was a great failure we all
breathed a sigh of relief—I'm sure Murray did too—that we could do
it to the Tchaikovsky. Everybody loves that piece.

It's one of my favorites.

When my parents saw *Porcelain* (they try to see as much dance as they can but they don't get to see a whole lot) they thought it was superb.

Have they seen Scheherazade?

No, so they're going to be doubly thrilled when we do it in Denver.

Is that why Murray is doing it in Denver?

Yes, as a matter of fact. He's doing it in Denver because of my parents, which is nice. The last time we played Denver we did almost the whole repertory. We did two different programs there. So this time we give them *Scheherazade* two nights in a row. *If* there are enough people to fill the house two nights in a row.

Isn't Denver dance-oriented?

No, it's just started.

It's interesting that you've described Salt Lake City as being so dance-oriented and Denver is not. How does this happen?

Well, in Salt Lake City, Virginia Tanner has always worked there. Her girls started as tiny little tots and went clear through high school taking dance from her, and she taught an improvisational, creative approach to dance. Then Elizabeth Hayes came to the University of Utah maybe twenty-five years ago and was very strong. She was a student of Margaret H'Doubler's at the University of Wisconsin and Margaret H'Doubler was *the* teacher of all the dance education pioneers in this country. Elizabeth Hayes carried on in Utah to such great effect that the girls who graduated out of Virginia Tanner's classes could then come right to the university there, and continue.

These girls would get their teaching certificate and go out and start dance programs in the high schools in Salt Lake City, and high school kids would become interested and then they'd go to Utah. Also, the Utah Civic Ballet [now Ballet West] was centered there. They have their yearly *Nutcracker,* which gets everybody interested. And there's a very large theater program at the University and a great tradition of going to the theater.

But there really must be a conducive atmosphere because even with great dance teachers it doesn't happen in every place.

The Mormons have a tradition of going to the theater and to the dance. That's mainly why it has prospered and grown there, along with the genius of the teachers at Utah.

Joan Woodbury and Shirley Ririe created much of the excitement that made the modern dance department at Utah such a success. Certainly they were our ideals when we were studying there. Their enthusiasm for what they were doing was so inspiring. That's what every teacher should have for dance and there's so little of it around the country. It's too bad. But those two just enthused and got us enthused. It worked both ways. The nice thing about Utah is that the dance majors can cross the boundaries. The modern dancers take ballet classes and the ballet dancers take modern classes, and get other points of view. That's extremely good. Rare too.

What attracted you first about the Nikolais technique? Why did you end up going to Nikolais instead of Merce Cunningham or Anna Sokolow?

Of the three people you mention, I had experienced all of them in my college career.

That's why I mentioned them. And you probably had more that you didn't mention.

At Utah Joan Woodbury and Shirley Ririe had been taking summer sessions with Nikolais for some time, so his thinking had been infused into their thinking, and Joan Woodbury had studied under Mary Wigman. At Utah they taught a spatial, abstract approach to dance, as opposed to a dramatic approach, and they taught very well. I was used to it when I first heard Nikolais speaking the pure word of all the experiences that I'd been having in college. When I heard Nikolais speak himself (and I've heard other people say the same thing) his articulation, his depth of understanding of his own material and his ability to say it and to make a student respond were astounding. No dance students ever expect their teachers to speak so well in order to get out of the students what they expect, and Nikolais is utterly unique that way. A lot of teachers rely on poetic imagery or musical imagery. They get at the movement experience through other means, whether literary or imagistic or however. But Nikolais puts his finger right on it and says it. It was heady, intoxicating, to hear this richness coming out of him, to hear the authority that he brought, to see it working in classes. When finally I took a summer session with him at Utah, I could conceive of no one else I wanted to study with.

Cunningham had been too early. I was only eighteen or nineteen when I took the Cunningham workshop. And while it was marvelous at the time, I hadn't any further contact with that technique, really. A few exercises—everybody does a few Cunningham exercises, I suppose. My ballet training at Utah had superseded my Cunningham technique—which I say because the Cunningham technique had codified itself almost as rigidly as the classical ballet technique, I think.

Even the Graham technique had codified itself into a certain range of steps, a certain way of doing things. They have become styles, as the ballet is a style of moving, and that's valuable to a dancer at a certain stage in his career. If you're going to be a Cunningham dancer, it's extremely valuable to know all that. If you're going to be a communicator on a more universal level, I think it's wise to have a wider range of experience in dance.

In the Nikolais technique you get down to such basics that you can claim universality for them. You work in the basics of motion—the sensing of the weight of a gesture, the time it takes, the space it encompasses. All dance uses these things, but not all dance speaks of them. If you are aware of these elements you use them sensitively and communicate with them much more readily. Too many techniques rely on the steps alone. You learn the steps and then voilá! you're a dancer. But it's just not so. All the greatest dancers are sentiently aware of the basics of motion even if they haven't ever said it in the front part of their brains.

As Murray says, the body and the muscles know these basic things. They have been inherited from hundreds of thousands of years of evolution. Western man ignores his body. He ignores the messages that are sent to his brain. And that's a form of death, because you're ignoring life. It's going for the abstraction rather than the reality. You settle for a dumb show, you settle for the shadow, you settle for doing the movement rather than getting underneath it, finding out what actually goes into the movement—the time of it, the shape of it, the notion of it, the energy employed. Or you learn one way of doing it and think that that is *the* way. And it's not. Dancers are so often naïve that way. That's one of the reasons some people say dancers are dumb, because even if they have learned different, dancers tend to say that one way is *the* way because someone they admire greatly has taught them that way, and they think they should shut out other ways of thinking.

What is the connection between the teaching of the Nikolais-Louis material and the performance of it? It's at such a high level in performance that when you go to see it you enter right into it and there's nothing getting in the way of this communication between the audience and the performer.

That's the marvelous secret of our technique. In any of our technique classes you learn physical skills for increasing your range of movement, for realizing a certain attack, a certain use of energy, a certain use of the body in unexpected or expanded ways. For example, we learn a cognizance of space. We are taught space for weeks and months on end—how to deal with the stuff outside the body. The area just beyond the fingertips, the area at the edge of the fingertips, the space between the arm and the torso, the space above the head, below the feet, underneath the floor. We're taught how to make geometrical shapes on space. How to draw a circle on the space and make an audience see it. How to make a circle with the arm and not have the audience see a circle on space but see an arm going in a circular way. All these little gradations of how to use space, of how to use the body, are taught in technique class.

When I started studying at the Henry Street Playhouse, Phyllis Lamhut taught Monday, Bill Frank taught on Tuesday, Nikolais taught on Wednesday, Gladys Bailin on Thursday, and Murray Louis on Friday. You had one class from each of them in a week, which has never been equalled and never will be again because the touring was not in force then; everyone stayed home all the time, so you had continuity, and the students benefited. They reaped the incredibly rich harvest of all the research that Nikolais and his small core of dedicated dancers did. They learned on their own bodies. Nikolais verbalized it, and then it was taught to the students.

Then the touring came along and the companies left on tour. There was always someone there to teach the classes, but there were no reserves to dip into. For several years running, there was some student discontent because they weren't getting the strong thing that had been there before. But then after a while Phyllis no longer danced with Murray and she started teaching regularly at the studio.

This was after the Playhouse; we'd gone to the "Space" on Thirty-sixth Street by the time Phyllis was teaching regularly. Whenever the companies were in town, company members would teach and Nikolais and Murray would teach also. Now I think the students are more content. I really don't have a great deal of contact with students because we're out of town so much.

Is there a difference between a Nikolais class and a Louis class?

At the School the students are already grounded in the technique or they are learning the basics of the technique in a coherent fashion over a period of time. Nikolais is so extremely specific and very demanding that what he's talking about is what he gets. He makes his students perform spatially, perform timewise, perform energywise according to the intellectual theory which he has architecturally set up in his head. He insists that his students work in class in that fashion.

Murray is different. He is always striving to make the class take off by working with a certain technical point or a certain point of principle, but working through enthusiasm and through getting the energy out, almost as if it were a performance for an audience. In class, Murray will choreograph a phrase, a combination, emphasizing the direction or dimension *up*—the student learns the phrase and as he goes across the floor he is told to feel *upwardness*. Thus the body is already going up as the intellect recognizes what is happening. Nik, on the other hand, will make the student stand at the end of the room before beginning the combination and say to him, now *be* up, show me your upwardness. O.K., now *as* you do the movement, imbue it with the upwardness you now have. Don't let yourself rest from your state of height.

Is this clear? With Murray the mechanics come first, the awareness later. With Nik the concept is first and foremost; a *willing* of the body by the mind to conform to an ideal. Both methods work; Murray's is more fun, more dancy, although Nik would disagree because to him the state of dance awareness is from the intellect, while to Murray it is from the viscera.

Murray is a marvelous teacher because his enthusiasm is communicated to the dancers. Nikolais makes you think about what you're doing. He insists that the intellectual preparation go along with the physical preparation. In that way you can approach a performance on the stage assured that you know what you are doing, because you have experienced it in your body both ways. Murray will let the intellectual go in favor of the energy coming out and happening. In a way they're both right. Nikolais's benefit is obvious. I mean if everything is going you know what is happening and you can do it. Obviously that will work. Murray's way is a bit more chancy but he trusts the body to learn those things by itself without going through a literal speaking of the words to the mind.

I'm not saying that Nikolais doesn't teach stimulating classes. I find, having worked with Murray for so long, that I swing completely to his way of thinking about things and it almost irritates me to take a Nikolais class because of the way he approaches a new problem—a problem of dynamics or a combination of steps. He'll think it out intellectually and say, "It should work this way, if you do it in such and such a way." You throw yourself into it or play with it, as it develops during the class, and still you find you cannot do the movement. Let me explain further.

Nikolais is fond of having you swing out in one way, then suddenly stop and turn in an unexpected way, and he says if you do it in a certain way it can work; he can see that in his eye and think it in his mind. But dancers, traditionally I suppose, like to turn off that reasoning, analytical faculty and just let the movement take it. So it's difficult for them to change gears in the middle and make a fine adjustment to dynamics or body weight in order to have this thing happen. That's happened to me time and time again in Nikolais classes. I get frustrated as hell because I can't let out fully all the time. But again, I've had wonderful Nikolais classes.

Murray said that his work with Nik made him stretch his body in all kinds of ways he never would have done on his own—that he never would have had the patience or the energy or the thought to do.

True, and in that sense I feel guilty because I feel that I should be able to go through the discipline of the Nikolais approach. I did for three years, and learned a great deal, but I consider myself a primarily physical being. So Murray's way appeals to me a great deal. It's an intuitive, muscular reaction—spontaneous—as in improvisation. That's joy to me. I always feel that I'm living most intensely when I'm on stage doing that. Even with the structure of the piece set and the steps set, other things are left open to improvisation. A lot of the timing, all the transitions from one thing to another are left open to the dancer, and you can play with that from performance to performance. That may seem like a very small thing but it's intensely satisfying to do. Even in the same piece, over and over.

Can you give an example of Murray's way?

An example that's obvious but may be a little misleading is the duet in *Hoopla* between Murray and myself. In the beginning Murray had only the idea of showing two performers giving each other the confidence to present themselves and also drawing confidence from the cheering of the crowd, then showing how sometimes one thing or the other is not enough. Or, you can't rely on the bolstering outside yourself to be a performer, you have to have it inside yourself. So he choreographed this very strange duet of one person egging another on. We showed the first version to Nikolais and he said, "It doesn't quite work. You should switch places occasionally," because as originally choreographed I was always the one who was doing the egging on and he was always the one who was egged. So Murray switched it around and sometimes I was the one who was being egged and sometimes I was the egger.

We went on the boards with it; it was always a low point during the first few months of *Hoopla* because neither of us knew what that duet was about. We knew the vague subject matter but we had no idea how to play it. It was only after playing it many times in front of many audiences that we began to get a sense of what it was actually all about and how to play the thing. Murray became an extremely erratic, dramatic figure in the performance between the two of us. He was always doing something that I wasn't expecting and he was always doing it in a dramatic way, which is not what we're trained in. I saw what he was doing and I stuck strictly to the steps and became a very strong figure, a wall that he was battering against. He would lapse into looking around the stage and trying to pull the inspiration out of some place.

We played it that way for a long time, maybe a year. Then this past fall it got amorphous, the dynamics of it got strange again, and I knew the old way of playing it was dead. It was not working the way it had been. I could tell from the audience reaction. I could tell because Murray was trying new things and I was trying to hang on to my old character, and the thing was not clicking. This lasted all through the recent New York season [December 20, 1974–January 5,

1975] and I felt badly that it went on that way but I didn't know what to do. Then on this tour a new thing has come out, in which I have started to take on a bit of his erratic, dynamic quality. I get too high at my high points and too low at my low points, which is what he has been doing all along, and this has started to work very interestingly and in a new way. It's very different. Anyone who had only seen the first performance of it and saw it now would not recognize it.

I've never understood it properly until the performance last night.

It's about performing and the bolsterings and the need for applause. It's a very sad duet, and a lot of people wonder why this sad little vignette is in the middle of this funny, happy piece. But it's really quite a keystone moment in *Hoopla.* All of *Hoopla* is about performing and performers, their hopes and fears, how things don't work, having to have the strength to pull it out of yourself, and insisting that it come out in a certain way to the audience. That's what *Hoopla* is about, besides being a very entertaining, funny dance.

Sort of the bright side versus the inside.

The inside which is not always so bright. People always need more than one viewing of it to see that. Although they do get an odd note in the first viewing and they say, "There's something strange in it that I didn't catch the first time around."

But that's good.

That's very good. You can go and see it as a circus ballet and take the kids and everybody will have a good time. That's all right too. We used to do an abridged version for kiddie matinees but we don't any more. Our kiddie matinee days are over, I think.

What about teaching? Do you like to teach?

Yes, I enjoy teaching the master classes. I don't enjoy teaching over a period at our School. I think of a class as almost another kind of performance where you have a certain captive bunch of people and you direct their energies in a certain way, and vibrations are given off in both directions. Teaching a long workshop or a series of classes, you have to have your mind organized and be intellectually grounded in the material. Characteristically, I don't like to be that organized. I like to be spontaneous, and I thoroughly enjoy a class when everything comes together and there's a lot of excitement—like what happened in the class here in Moscow. That was fulfilling to me because everybody enjoyed it. I enjoyed teaching it, and even Murray came and said it was a very nice class.

If I ever decide to teach instead of perform, I would have to spend some quiet time deciding and organizing in my mind and probably even writing down what I would teach. Otherwise I don't know if I could trust myself to give a coherent linear development of the material. I know almost everything in the technique and the theory, but I think my body knows it more than my mind has articulated it. Whenever Murray says a thing I say, "That's true." But I know it as a performer, not as a teacher. As a teacher you *must* be articulate, you have to be able to get it out and to say it. That's always been one of my problems. I've never been a good speaker. I've always been reticent and shy about having to say anything.

That's what I'm feeling teaching a course in dance history.

Yes. What do you say? You feel confident in your own material, but how do you communicate it pungently? I mean you can talk and talk and say absolutely true things, and everyone is yawning and falling asleep. But to say it interestingly or with enough wit and enough bite so that people pay attention . . .

Well, they did the other day in the class you taught.

Yes, but I'd had practice in that kind of thing. Also I'm around Murray Louis, who is the master of that kind of teaching and that kind of pungency. I attribute all of my teaching ability to observing Murray teach. All of it.

Teaching is an enormous responsibility.

Yes, so is learning. Most dancers only copy the step they see. They learn by repetition, which is anathema in our technique because it's mindless, it's unthinking, it's almost uncaring, it's only a result of the will to perfect a thing or to attain a kind of perfection, in order to prove that you as an individual can achieve this. A kind of exhibitionism, a kind of narcissism, a showing off.

I would say eighty-five percent of dance learning is in order to show off. Isn't that strange? I think a dancer's basic motivation is narcissistic. Maybe I'm speaking only of myself. The atmosphere is more palpable in some classes than others. In certain ballet classes the young girls who are studying wear flowers in their hair to class. That speaks to me of a certain missing of the point of what they're doing. It's skipping the life experience in order to achieve the glamour of the stage moment. It's the unawareness that an intellectual thing has to happen. They mistake decor for the art, and the teachers foster that.

Are you speaking of ballet now, or of all dance?

I'm speaking of most dance instruction. The teachers are either frustrated performers or ex-performers, and their dream or their memory of dance is of that ecstatic moment on the stage, that moment of communication. Too often that moment of communication is concerned with superficial things—glamour, pretty costumes, applause—and that moment feeds the teachers in their memories or in their anticipations, so they communicate that expectation to their students rather than the actual material of the art of dancing, or the art of motion.

I'm trying to keep my vocabulary as broad as possible, because in our specific technique when I say "motion" I mean a specific kind of experience. It's a very tight definition which is not shared by all dancers, by any means. Most dancers will speak of motion and movement interchangeably and we don't. Movement is just what you see—the arm lifted, the leg in a ronde de jambe. Motion is the finely sensed involvement with the movement, then on into the poetic, inner, communicative thing.

This definition of motion is crucial to our technique. In simple terms it can be explained by taking the example of two men walking down a street. One man is in a hurry—he walks with his head down, he doesn't realize where he is—he just knows he is going from point A to point B. The other man will walk with enjoyment in what he is doing. He senses the air, the sun on his face, and the people around him—he is alive to the moment. This man's awareness of what is going into his brain as he functions is what the dancer must have when he is dancing, when he is concerned with motion. It's an absolute second-by-second awareness. Motion is always concerned with the how and the now. It is never concerned with what's coming up or what has happened before.

Isn't motion then very much concerned with your own life experiences?

I was reading an article about William Carter ["Bill Carter: an Interview," by Tobi Tobias, *Dance Magazine,* June 1975] and he said that in the early years, the young dancer's energies and strengths lend themselves to an expression and a communication of vigor and enjoyment of the physical throwing oneself into life, which is joyful to see, and audiences love it. But later on in your career you cannot drive your body to the utmost limits which that kind of dancing demands. You begin to realize that the things that happen to you in life are as much a part of you as the movement experiences that you've had. You want to communicate through your chosen medium, which is dance, which is motion, the things you're finding out about life and about existence—the common, universal experiences of mankind, the realizations and the revelations that you've had about what you've experienced and their relationship to other people. So you find that this spectacular technique you've acquired is not serving what you want to do, and you have to go a little deeper into your own experience in order to expand your physical range—not more spectacular things but signposts along the way of experience. You have to find a way that movement communicates more than just joie de vivre, a way that movement communicates more than simple love or simple lust, or as Nikolais used to say, "sad, mad, glad." Experience is much richer than just these youthful expressions. You find out that what has been taught to you in the classroom isn't enough. You have to go deeper.

What's nice about Murray is that he's already leading us on in these directions, pushing us on in his new choreographies. Building on what we can do, he pushes us on into a slightly different set of mind about the way a thing is performed. This makes you think; how is my life experience related to this? It's almost impossible not to think of these things. The only way is to set up defenses and say, this doesn't interest me and I'm not going to do it any more. Then it's time to pull back, maybe get out of the heavy performing for a while, think your own thoughts, go off in a corner. For a year Phyllis Lamhut left the Nikolais company and danced in off-Broadway shows. Then she came back because she decided that the richness was where she had been. But she had to get away in order to think, to realize, to make a contrast. If you're brought up on vichysoisse, you don't realize what stew is. You don't realize the richness of what you have.

William Carter danced in Martha Graham's pieces and

discovered a whole new vocabulary, a whole new way of moving. More important, he discovered that there were ways to express what he himself was feeling about life. He says that Graham actually rechoreographed old roles for him, which is a remarkable thing, considering the strength of a person like Graham. Well, she was confident enough in her own strength to do that for someone else, someone she may have been a little less sure of, or someone who was not quite so tried as the originator of the role might have been. She was willing to mine the resources of a new individual in the same role.

Only a few great people have enough conviction in their own endeavor to do that for another person—to pull out of another person what the person can give or to force that person to plumb his own self in order to contribute to the work at hand. Murray does that. I'm sure Graham did that. The young Graham dancers seem to be technically astounding, but they don't have the intensity of the old dancers, and I would say the intensity is necessary. They need that conviction to get across the dream that Graham conceived.

Many of them are in the throes of youth still, so they're getting at something else.

I'm sure she had more mature dancers with her, as well as a newer crop, when she had her first programs. I'm sure Erick Hawkins was no kid when she started using him in her pieces.

There's
something
magic about
a banana
split

Touring: food, keeping your sanity,
living the moment

Moscow, continued.

How do you feel about touring?

That's an interesting subject. It has taken me a long time to get used
to touring. I have been doing it almost steadily since the spring of
1967. At first I didn't understand what was going on. Now, having
toured so much, I can see that in addition to all the new situations
which touring forces upon you, you live on different levels of energy.
There is touring energy and performing energy and
being-in-New-York-and-rehearsing energy.

People who travel with us sometimes do not understand.
Someone who is along on a tour will tell us we're a bunch of
fuddy-duddies because we won't go to the cathedral, but everybody
says, "Maybe we'd better not, maybe we'll just stay in our rooms."
That's hard for a tourist to understand, but one who is performing
has to ration his energy. On a tour you are performing in the
evenings and so your days tend to be quiet, not filled with walking
and seeing cathedrals and going to museums because you know that
you'll wear yourself out and your basic energy will be drained into
those concrete sidewalks rather than saved for the performance.

The performance is a gigantic push. There's the whole thing of
getting yourself prepared for the performance, pulled up to a certain
level where the molecules within you are ready to go out. You stretch
your body, you get it warmed and ready, the blood is circulating in a
special way, taking more care of the muscles than it usually does when
you're not dancing.

You have to prepare the psyche too. Makeup is an important ritual in accomplishing this. You need to spend that time quietly, without a lot of racket going on in order to pull your head together and go through certain automatic actions, putting on the face while the energies coalesce. All of this takes a lot of concentrated energy and so it's wonderful to have a day off like today where we are not confined by a schedule, and we can spend our energies in different ways without saving them for the big push in the evening.

In other words touring energy is conditioned by performing energy. The performances are the key.

Right. And all this adds up to a special touring energy and set of mind. I remember my first years of touring. I was a nervous wreck. I think particularly with one like me who's so very shy and out of contact with a lot of people and a lot of situations, I didn't realize what was the matter with me. I just knew I was unhappy and I didn't know whether it was an excess of nerves or an excess of stimuli coming in and dumping on me or what kind of insecurity it was. Maybe that's what maturity is, finding out what those things are.

Finding out and not being ashamed of them but accepting them.

Right. Accepting them, but I think even before that you have to find out what is happening. Then you can go about accepting them.

Touring must really make you do that.

Yes, it's forced upon you. Touring is a crazy life—sometimes you can be so tired you have to grit your teeth.

Is it weariness from throwing things into a suitcase, going to the airport, going to the hotel, and going on the bus to and from the airport? That can really wear you down.

Travelling is very wearing. Even if I didn't have to throw things into a suitcase and get to the airport, there's something about jet travel itself: the waiting for the plane; getting on the plane; experiencing the up and down; the ear changes; the atmospheric pressure changes; holding yourself in a little seat for that length of time. It's wearing in a physical way—a muscular way. People don't realize that unless they travel a lot. An airline seat is rather narrow and you can't spread yourself lest you nudge your neighbor. You're using muscles to keep your elbows in toward you, or your knees together, rather than letting yourself sprawl as you would in an easy chair. And waiting for the baggage and waiting for the plane to take off. Waiting takes energy also.

All that accumulates, so two days off in a row is a big treat if you're in one place, where you don't have to unpack, travel or do anything, and you don't have a schedule. Particularly like now, in the middle of a tour. It's necessary. If you don't get it, you feel it.

I have been reading *Future Shock* [by Alvin Toffler] and it has given me interesting insights into the pattern of my life in that his whole book is about the adaptability of mankind to new situations. My life fit his description perfectly in being a continual confrontation with new situations. Not only in performing—always a new audience every night, which could be a very contained kind of daily confrontation—but touring too. There's always a new city and there are always new people to meet. And after a while you are so bombarded by this you start to say, "I don't want any more." Unconsciously your mind gets fuzzy and you start to be absentminded and you don't remember people's faces. You block out new stimuli because you have had your fill.

At home I have a very stable life and I have to keep it that way. Toffler says you have to have some stability somewhere in your life or you just go loony. I didn't know that before, but now I can see it consciously and see how it happened without my even knowing it. Because on the road my professional life is so erratic.

Do you feel differently about touring now than you did in the beginning?

I don't mind touring now. I like to get out of New York City. I think if I had to live in New York twelve months a year I'd go absolutely insane, the energy there is so insistent. And it's nice to be able to get out to Idaho and sit in a motel room and nothing is happening and only Johnny Carson on television, and you can glory in nothing new happening. And at the same time, I'm dancing, which is what I love doing, and so I feel almost as if I had the best of all possible worlds because I'm doing what I love doing and I'm earning a living doing it. I don't have to do it as a side line and I get a good enough balance of change and stability.

*How does this tour [six weeks in the Western part of the United
States, Canada, and Florida] compare with others?*

It is going along almost like any other tour, and being used to
touring, we know we can put up with six weeks of it without undue
mental strain or emotional stress. After the six-week mark you begin
to get a little crazy, to become more reclusive. You draw away from
company functions. You try to stay away from parties and from things
that haven't much to do with the performances and you begin to
value your private time a lot more.

   Sometime when a tour goes on too long you just get vegetative.
Like one of our recent European tours. It was too long and Murray
knows that too. We got on the bus to go to the airport and he said,
"Oh golly, nine weeks." And I said, "Murray, it's an eleven-week
tour," and he said, "No, no, no it's only nine weeks," and I said,
"Murray, it's an eleven-week tour," and he said, "What? I told them
no more than eight weeks at the outside and I figured it would
probably be nine." Now we're up for a South American tour, next
spring, and he says it'll only be six weeks long and I'm just waiting for
that tour to shape up. And I'm gritting my teeth because I don't
want to go to South America. I have no interest in South America. I
don't want to go there.

Well, that's a pre-conceived notion. It's fascinating, parts of it.

Okay. I just don't want to go. We'll play all the big cities. We'll be
doing big opera houses and theaters.

*And Argentina and Buenos Aires—a cosmopolitan city, with fabulous
steaks.*

Mmm. Another steak. Do you know Kitty, in the Midwest that's all
you can eat in restaurants because you daren't eat anything else
because THESE PEOPLE DON'T KNOW HOW TO COOK.

I wanted to talk about food.

Food in the American restaurant is in a ghastly state. I guess it always
has been. Alan Watts, the writer and philosopher, has an interesting
point. He says that for a people who have been accused of being
materialists Americans care very little for the material that surrounds
them. Their food is plastic, their motel furniture is plastic.

Like this motel lamp.

Do you see that it is even nailed down to the table? So many of the
materials that surround Americans are inferior. They give no joy. The
design is dull, it is standardized and cheap to make. It's ugly. It's
cheap, and that has been the factor which feeds us, which clothes us,
which houses us—the economic factor, the cheapness of the
production. Watts says in that sense Americans are certainly not
materialists. They are worshippers of abstractions, they are worshippers
of money which is an abstract symbol for real wealth. Real wealth is
food to eat and clothes to wear and a roof over your head, and if you
go for money it's like spending your life writing columns of figures.
It's a purely abstract goal which gives you no comfort unless you take
a miser's comfort in numbers.

Do you find when you go around the country, that people are hungry
for some kind of aesthetic that you can give them?

Genuine thing? Oh yes. Absolutely. Most people are just bowled over
by our concerts because we give them the real thing. We give them a
genuine moment in which we are not putting anything on. We're not
trying to bamboozle them in any way. We're presenting what we are
and what we believe in without a veneer. We don't tell them they
should do anything. We only present and let them draw their own
conclusions. And that's so refreshing because there is so much
phoniness, particularly in the arts.

The phoniness is just overwhelming. It's like this formica table
top. It's a defense. People without any real aesthetic or artistic
sensibility hide behind the aesthetic pose and it works on the average
American because the average American is so little exposed to the
genuine thing. People are intimidated into believing that they are
receiving an artistic experience because first of all it's an unfamiliar
experience to them. I'm talking about dance now, the dance
experience is unfamiliar to them, but now that dance is opening out
in the country they see more and I think they're beginning to be
bamboozled less and less because more and more people talk about
the "unsatisfactory experience they had with 'X' dance company
which played here last spring." And they talk about how satisfying our
performance is.

I don't say out of just egocentricity that I think we're the greatest thing in the world, aside from the fact that I do think we're the greatest thing in the world. People are hungry for the real thing and I think particularly now, when everything has blown up in the air, people will start to insist on the real thing, I hope in all phases of life—a real relationship with another person, rather than a marriage and a home because that is what is expected. I think people would rather have a real relationship with a person and serve real food lovingly prepared (this is quoting from Alan Watts whom I admire immensely) and not go for the plastic and not settle for the symbol of something rather than the actual thing itself. We don't need the fancy restaurant in which you get an extremely attractively prepared meal which tastes like nothing because it's been made with chemicals.

Have meals changed over the years?

No. I think that will change last. America has to give up its obsession with the dollar as a symbol. And that's going to take a long time. It'll be beyond our lifetimes. I have no hope for American food. The steaks are maybe the best you get because people spend more time on them.

Steak is a status symbol.

Exactly. But the roast turkey dinner, the pork chops, even the frankfurter, it's just ugh! You can kid yourself with a hamburger because they more or less all taste the same, you don't have to see the way it actually looks. But how many steaks and how many hamburgers can you eat on a tour?

I find I hit points where I can't eat anything and I'm hungry, but I know if I eat something I will gag. Fortunately I've found the solution. I have a banana split, instead of an entire meal. And usually it works because, I don't know, there's something magic about a banana split.

America cares about banana splits. Not in the chain stores but in an ice cream parlor we do. Here's another thing that has struck me. Everyone has to spend so much energy finding these little places, like the health food store of the town or the ice cream parlor of the town.

Or the place that serves a decent meal at eleven at night. I guess you have to accept that as part of touring. Food is important to the

dancer because it's the fuel that's burned when you're giving off that
kind of energy, so it has to be on a certain level. You can't eat french
fries and pizza all the time. Even with a banana split, most times the
banana is green and you can't win for losing.

*I notice you have to say, "Please bring real milk" with the coffee, and
if you don't say that—*

It comes propylene glycol or whatever the hell that stuff is.

But wherever you are a lot of time is spent on food.

It's very important to the dancer. You see, it's not so important to
other people and that's the problem. The nutritionists lately, Adelle
Davis and those people, have said that Americans are so well fed that
they don't pay any attention to what they're eating or the taste of it
or the texture of it. If they were wiser about the quality of the food
they ingested they would take more care of how it was prepared and
food in general would become a lot more enjoyable.

*I would like to ask you what you pack in your suitcase for a tour. It's
sort of a silly question.*

No, it's not silly at all. First you find out where you're going; then
you have to pack a variety of things. For this tour we are playing
Canada and Nebraska and very northern places and Tampa, Florida.
We are going to Mexico too, but I didn't have to pack for Mexico
because I go home for a few days before we go there.

I have a list which stays in my suitcase all the time whether the
suitcase is in use or not. And this list is the basics I must carry no
matter where I go. I have several categories. The first category is
dance clothes, and under that I have leotards, tights, dance belts,
rehearsal clothes, a towel, and woolly socks. The second category is
dress clothes: jacket, slacks, dress shoes, a tie, a dress shirt if I need it.
On this tour I didn't bring any of that because I didn't plan on going
anyplace. My third category is what I call "clothes clothes" which are
jeans, T-shirts, socks, underwear, sweaters, sweatshirts, things like that.
My fourth category is toiletries and I have a list of everything,
toothbrush and all that business. Then I have a sundry list; my
address book, galoshes, and odd things that don't fit under other
categories like books because I don't want to be trapped someplace
without anything to read. That happens sometimes.

What do you bring for books?

On this tour I brought Christopher Isherwood's *Berlin Stories,* Anita Loos's *Gentlemen Prefer Blondes,* Thomas Hardy's *Jude the Obscure,* Tolstoy's *Anna Karenina* which I've read before but which I think is time to read again, *Future Shock,* Alan Watts's autobiography *In My Own Way,* and *The Prince in Waiting,* which is a fantasy book. I try to strike a balance between light things and heavy things. But while I'm on tour I always pick up other books because I'm an inveterate bookstore browser. I don't like to stick to any one category in my reading. Also I don't get to read too much in New York, there are so many other things to do. So I do most of my reading on the road. It's a good pastime.

I've started writing on this tour. I hit a hotel room where I was dead struck dumb with nothing to do and I started to write an epic narrative poem which is part of a fantasy story that's been going through my head, vaguely, for the past fifteen years. I've been writing sections of it and destroying them and writing other sections and losing them and so I decided to write a new section in poetry form. I started on that and I finished about fifteen pages of legal pad size and stopped. I haven't felt the urge to continue.

And you have your crazy little things. You go out and eat something you shouldn't just because you have to do it. Or, you spend energy in a way that you probably shouldn't because it might detract from the performance. Like getting into the hot pool in Sun Valley, which completely saps your energy. You get out of it a limp rag and you would think that that would just be death on the day of a performance but I found it relaxed me and I still had plenty of energy for the performance.

Hot water is such an incredible invention. Americans have to be commended for making hot water the norm, particularly in our profession. Hot water relaxes tense muscles. It's a release mechanism to get into a hot shower and stay there and stay there and stay there, because it's a sensuous experience along your body and it's relaxing your muscles and it's private and it's just kind of nice in there. So I enjoy showers. When I'm really down I just hop into a shower and I feel better. Over the years you find what makes you feel better.

*What makes different things stand out on tour? What do you
remember?*

I remember not so much what happened as how I felt about things.
Maybe it's part of a repression-release mechanism. There are certain
times when I have enjoyed a perfectly ordinary experience
extraordinarily. Something has clicked where the environment or
what's going on has released great joy or great feeling of some kind in
me. And I think that's what I remember from all those years of
touring.

I remember the first European tour of Nikolais's. We went to
Yugoslavia. At one performance I broke my little toe as I ran off stage
and jammed it into a lead weight that was sitting on the floor. At the
time I wasn't admitting to myself that it was broken. I only knew
that it was very sore and I couldn't wear a shoe because it was very
swollen. Anyway, I was in kind of a funk from that. But we hit a
small town in the mountains, Sarajevo in Yugoslavia, which was
getting toward the south, so there began to be a Muslim culture
which was totally unfamiliar to us. We were going to take a little bus
trip to a nearby springs or park or something like that. And I
remember we were driving in this rather small bus and it had a
window on top, a tinted window rather than a solid ceiling. And we
were driving through fields which were ploughed on either side of us.
And suddenly the road turned and there was a straight avenue
between some very tall trees which arched over the road. These trees
were just planted bing, bing, bing along the road. The driver was
driving fairly slowly, for some reason, through this avenue and I was
just miserable and I was lying there and I started to look up and these
trees were over us and the fields were being ploughed on either side
of us between these regularly spaced columns and I had such a rush
of joy that it was an indescribable experience. Tears started running
down my cheeks and I started dabbing away and hoping nobody was
seeing me, but I was just having this indescribable experience.

That's the kind of thing I remember, rather than meeting
Sargent Shriver in Paris at an Embassy party or something like that.
Even the performances tend to blend into each other because there
are so many similar elements in them. Performances I think I block
off in my mind, as the absolute momentary thing, that one moment
when the energy of the audience and our energy happens all together

into an experience. And that is almost encapsulated as the reason for what I'm doing, and I keep that just as that, and I don't feed off that in my own personal emotional life or my mental memory process. Because I know it's ongoing. I don't have to remember fondly when we played for the queen of such and such.

Is it physical environment that you remember?

What I remember is my reaction—it's not *what* it is, it's the reaction. Because that's what plants itself in my memory cells. Although environment is probably what triggers it. Or great emotional stress, such as when Murray's first company was starting to break up and people were starting to withdraw and there was no communication. I remember when I couldn't talk to certain people any more. They were having to pull themselves out of this situation because they were going to have to continue their own life afterwards and that was very painful. But that was just a human situation. That can happen to anyone.

Otherwise it all blends in.

It really does. I put great stress into living the moment. I don't hang on to memories. I really don't anticipate the future very much so I really try to get as much as possible out of the moment right now. And I don't fear for the future, when I'm too old to dance or some terrible accident will happen. Because if that happens life goes on and things take care of themselves.

And also I always feel that I've been terribly lucky because almost everything good has been handed to me. Falling right into the Nikolais company as soon as I came to New York, getting into Murray's company rather than staying with Nikolais's company. I felt myself learning within my craft as I was going along but the great things, the good things were just given to me, because I didn't expect or I didn't wish for them. I didn't expect them and I didn't yearn for them and I didn't try and so they just came, and it's very pleasant that they just happened. And in that sense I don't make any plans for the future. I don't say that when I'm finished dancing I'm going to be a teacher. Because as far as I know I could turn a corner into some completely different area of life.

Chapter
three

We always
must know
the how of
what we are
doing

Principles of the Nikolais-Louis
technique and
improvisation, transitions, nuance

An opportunity to join the Murray Louis Dance
Company on tour came in Saratoga Springs, N.Y.
Down the street from the motel was a small
cemetery. Michael and I went there to talk,
undisturbed except for a flock of raucous crows.

Would you like to talk about some of the principles of the
Nikolais-Louis technique?

There's the big five: space, time, shape, motion, and energy. Energy
was not on that list when I came to the Henry Street Playhouse, but
it has since been added. *Space* is the part of the universe where the
body isn't—in other words, it's everything outside your skin. But
Murray also talks about the space inside the body. You must be aware
of your space at all times. Unless in some particular piece you should
have a particular reason to ignore it. Because the body occupies space
and because it is a sentient instrument it obviously has to be aware of
the area outside of it, the space around it.

The German technique [Rudolf von Laban and Mary Wigman]
from which ours is descended put great emphasis on directions in
space: forward-going, backward-going, up and down, and all that
business—architectural constructions of the space sideways, front and
back, up and down, and also circles within this area around you.
Hanya Holm and Nikolais expanded it into a space far away from you

which you can manipulate. Obviously you can get your arm around a chunk of close space and show the audience a circle, or a beach ball, full of space which really isn't there—but it is. It exists because the performer's energy is focused into it. Far space is made visible to the observer's eye because the performer's energy is reaching out to the far space. Or you can reach just to the ends of your fingertips and draw lines on space, circles on space, or to the tip of the toe or tip of the knee.

Murray went into inner space with a sense of the body's being hollow, with just a few molecules floating around inside, and you can send all these molecules into one part of the body and make it much denser than the rest of the body. You can have the energy flowing through you from the tip of the right toe up through the right side of the body, up out the right arm, or crisscross, or however you want to do it. You can increase the number of molecules and move densely and heavily as if you weighed quite a bit, or you can move lightly with only one molecule bouncing around in you.

All these are aspects of spatial concern. The dancer shows the audience the space around him and the space inside him by virtue of his own concentration and belief in that space.

Since the seventeenth century, a performer's *time* has been a musical time divided into pulse: beat, beat, beat, beat. The dancer performed within that beat also. In the twentieth century it was discovered that music didn't necessarily have to conform to that four/four or three/four beat or variations thereof. The body of course is not a piano, it's an extremely complex instrument with muscles and nerves and tendons and its own time sense has really nothing to do with the four/four or the three/four except perhaps a walk is chum, chum, chum, chum one foot after the other, which would virtually make it into a two. Or the heart beat is ka-tum, ka-tum, ka-tum, which is almost a three rhythm, one-two-three, one-two-three. But these are variable. You don't have to walk in a two rhythm, your heart can speed up and slow down greatly. The body's timing, the muscles, have had nothing really to do with a musician's one-two and one-two-three.

So the concept of time began to be, *how long* does a movement take? *How long* does a gesture or a series of gestures take? Time became duration rather than pulse or musical phrases, durational phrases rather than counted phrases, I think. Generally speaking that's the biggest distinction that's been made in time. Time also involves the idea of timing, which is knowing when a thing is supposed to happen, a distinction between how long it should happen and when it should happen. Comedians have always known that timing is of the essence in their art, because whether you say the words with the right or wrong timing will decide whether or not the audience will laugh. And the dancer is said to have wit when his timing is precise and most pungent and most relative to the material that he's doing.

Shape is the body's sense of itself in a sculptural sense. The dancer as sculptor must be aware of his body's shape at all times. Sometimes the shape sense excludes the time sense, the space sense, and it becomes simply a statue, or it can twist itself into really quite abstract shapes. There is a very special feeling on your skin and right underneath your skin, when you are in that shape sense, which is impossible to verbalize. You do have a very special sense, a feeling (we call it texture) on the surface of the skin when you are in a shape sense because you are utterly ignoring the space outside you. You are simply concerned with body.

So much of dancing is taught in a shape sense, perfecting the line. Dancing is therefore taught in front of mirrors, and dancers become accustomed to looking in the mirror to see if they're making the right shape. They may not even realize that they're doing a shape thing. They just know that a certain look is correct and a certain look is not correct. That's a shape sense. And therefore they become bound in their flesh, all their dynamics are bound at skin level. When they go into a leap the thing that the viewer remembers seeing is the legs spread apart, the arms wide, the chin up in the air. That's the picture the viewer remembers, rather than having a sense of movement through the air, which is at least as important a part of a leap as the shape that the body has made in the air—that sense of thrust which the muscles automatically make but which the dancer can ignore or emphasize as he chooses.

In the case of a lot of dancing, all they want you to see is the gorgeous shape they make, the split second when they are in the air. That's what the audience remembers, because that's what the dancer wants to be seen—that shape. It's a pity. I blame a lot of what I call French dancing, sex dancing, on that preoccupation with just the body and nothing around it. If you get two people together with just their bodies there's almost immediately a sexual connotation. Whereas in real human experience there's an infinite variety of communications and of relationships between two people which can have more or less or nothing of sex connected with them. Why dance should be so bound to a sexual expression is a great source of wonder to me. Maybe it's just part of the sexual revolution. Maybe after dance goes through its sex phase it will go on to other less obvious relationships.

What is the difference between shape and space when you can make the same physical arm gesture for both things?

When you hold your arms in a circle in front of you, you have two elements. You have the arms in a circular shape and you have a round space which is bounded by the arms. How can a dancer make the difference clear enough so that the audience knows this is a circular shape of the arms or this is a circular space?

It has to do with the dancer's concentration and his use of energy. The shape sense is completely within the skin. The dancer's energy is held within the limits of his physical being, his skin, his bones, his muscles. He can show that roundness. It's probably even more obvious if he moves the shape to over his head or to one side and he can show that fairly rigid sense of a sculpture. It's as if you were to imagine that your arms were made of stone. That density of the energy within the arms as opposed to the rare density of the space.

So what you want me to notice is the arm shape, not the space inside the arms.

The muscle and skin—the shape. I, by virtue of my eye focus as well, can show you the shape of the arms rather than the shape of the space inside the arms. But wait. If I want to show you that circular space inside my arms, I let my arms be a lot easier, the energy within the arms becomes more fluid. My psychic sense begins to be more on the surface of my skin and emanating out from my skin so that I begin to show you the energy here. My eye focus goes to the space inside, and you see a round hole rather than the round shape of the arms.

Murray makes an explosive point about dynamic emphasis *(Glances)*. (*l. to r.:* Helen, Michael, Bill, Murray)

What we're talking about now in our vocabulary is the volume of the space, the area of space close to the body which you can surround with the parts of your body. These are volumes you can make, as opposed to outer space beyond the limits of your body, over there by that tree or clear out to the moon. That's the far space. You send the energy clear from your inner sources way out beyond. It involves the whole body. Any time that you're making anything you involve the whole body, but particularly in a space sense. All parts of the body have to contribute to the space that you're showing. You can't be making an arabesque and show the space between the fingers. It's not possible. Or suppose you're running and trying to show a space very close around you. A run is usually considered a cleaving of a larger space. If you want to show the close space while you're running you have to make it consonant by your concentration. It takes great concentration and great ability and great awareness of what you're trying to do. Because if you aren't aware that there's a contradiction in the first place when someone says, "Show me the space around you while you're running," you're lost.

Shape is within the flesh. Shape is always just the body. Space is around the body or outside the body or inside the body, but it is not the body.

Can shape be two bodies? Or twenty-five bodies?

Of course. In our lecture/demonstrations we make shapes with two bodies, and that's even more fascinating because you get greater variety with two bodies than with one—legs sticking out at odd angles.

When you're doing shape in yourself you're within your own flesh. Where does the concentration go when you have two people?

Same place. The way we work shape in our improvisation is that we have a shape, a statue. These two bodies making this shape. Then we have a transition period when we move through however many machinations and arrive at another shape. Then we stop and show you that shape. That's one very obvious way. Now, at the moments when we are still and we are showing you the shape, we have within ourselves this very strong, dense, shape sense. When it comes time to change, to do the transition, we let go of that density, watch each other carefully, pull off each other, hold on to each other, or get close, or get far, until we find out where the next shape is. Then we hit it and take the shape.

   You don't have to make yourself less dense, you can keep the dense texture in your body and still move. But when you keep your density the same you have to make every last minisecond as fascinating a shape as the one before it. You never arrive at a shape; you are always in shape. I suppose it's like a Henry Moore mother and child. But they are always a sculpture. That's very difficult; it takes incredible concentration. What you do is simply redirect your energies toward a moving sense, then you go into a still sense, a held sense.

That makes much more sense to me.

Shape is always the most popular thing with audiences. It's the easiest thing to see. It just *is*. It's there in front of you, and also, I think most people are used to watching dance in the sense of shapes made, beautiful shapes, ideal shapes most of the time.

   Now we have *motion.* Movement, the gross movement, is the lifting of the arm. Motion is the sensing of the inside of the movement, the lifting of the arm, while the arm weighs a certain amount, through a certain amount of space, occupying a certain amount of time. Motion is the sensing of all these things at once while the movement is happening. Motion is immediate. It is very obvious when motion is not there, and it is not there most of the time, I'm sorry to say, in most dance performances. In our technique, in our performances on the stage, we try at all times to be in a state of motion in that sensed way. Always trying to be completely aware of what's going on.

   Now, you can sacrifice a sense of motion for a sense of shape, or a sense of time, or a sense of space. You can be so totally concerned with space that your movement—the fact that you run-run-leap, run-run-leap across the stage—is not important. During the run-run you are going level and during the leap you are going up and over. This is your spatial structure—level-level-over, level-level-over. As a performer you can make the audience see low-low-high, low-low-high rather than run-run-leap, run-run-leap—dancer running, leaping; dancer running, leaping. We say a run-run-leap is the largest thing that a single body can do on stage. So I suppose the motional sense of run-run-leap would be the sensing of the great dynamic push that it has to have, the splitting of the legs in the air and the largeness of it. All these things given almost equal balance would lend a motional quality to the run-run-leap.

Motion does not have to be large; it can be very small. It can also be confined to one part of the body while the rest of the body remains still but attentive to what's going on. A lot of dancers tend to hold their heads out of what they're doing. Their bodies can be dancing and their heads are held still or held aloof from what they're doing. One of the most irritating things to watch is when the eyes of the dancer go closed and you know he is indulging in the movement rather than bending the spine, bending the neck, getting all of the body involved in the *motional* thing that is going on. If the head is held out the truth of the movement is destroyed.

Motion is the hardest thing to talk about because it means quality, it means finding the balance of the how. All the other things have to do with *what,* but motion is *how.* If the dancer is unaware of how he's achieving what he's achieving, he's not in motion, he's simply doing the movement.

Like Murray's moving one eyebrow, that kind of thing?

But as he moves it, the whole rest of his body knows that he's doing it, and the audience sees that and knows that that's the intent.

Or those funny face things in Personnae.

That's the point of what we're doing at that moment, and so everything is involved with that thing.

But many dancers don't use the face as part of the body.

I think it might be as a reaction against a dramatic expressiveness. They've been taught that the face is the most dramatic part of the body, and when doing a particularly abstract dance they have to keep their faces out of it. Sometimes they do dramatic dance keeping their face out of it, which is a startling idea if you really think about it. Also it's a fear, because your face is a window to the soul. And many dancers dance as a defense. They dance to cover up, to hide behind the movement. If you're hiding behind movement you're certainly not lending yourself to it. But a dancer who does not lend himself to his movement also reveals himself. We all know tight-assed dancers. You don't even know quite what it is about them. You just know that they are not involved in what they are doing and you want them to release, somehow. That itself bespeaks a psychological set of mind. They are afraid of motion, afraid of movement even. I think they want to study a specific style or a specific kind of movement and feel comforted that this is the way it is. They cannot trust themselves to find out what the movement demands rather than what their attitude about themselves demands. So they dance their attitude about themselves rather than dealing with the material.

That's mirror dancing again.

Precisely. I hate mirrors. Every time we teach a master class we go in and all the kids are sitting on the floor facing the mirror, waiting to have a class. So we set up on the other side, facing them away from the mirror.

Now, last of all, *energy.* This is mostly Murray's thinking. He has almost concluded that all these other things can be called divisions of the uses of energy. The body is the instrument, and energy is the raw stuff that you are dealing with. It is the paint inside the tube before it comes out. Therefore *how* is almost *how the energy is used.* Is it used in a rigid shape-making way? Or is it used in a flowing way so that it comes from the inside of you out into the space around you? Or is it used in a dramatic way so that the energy paths inside you go through your emotional centers as well, and get you involved in a dramatic kind of expression?

I think in our technique now, or what Murray has more or less evolved with the company and what he teaches in master classes, is a sense of energy within the body going out into space. It's a feeling of the energy patterns coming out of the body and creating the forms in space rather than an insistence on the preexistence of a form in space which the body fulfills. In that sense the dancer is more the creator of something that already exists.

Now, how does improvisation fit into all this?

Improvisation is the second stage of the dancer's training in our technique, the first being the process of getting the body to respond the way you want it to. Murray explains improvisation as turning the tables around, listening to your body, finding out what it wants to do, what it wants to say, and *how* it wants to say it.

In our technique, improvisation puts the student in touch with his body and how it wants to move and how it's going to deal with motion. In improvisation you cannot move *except* spontaneously. If you move with deliberation, with an intellectual preconception, it shows immediately.

Through improvisation you connect your intellectual centers into an ancestral knowledge which has come down through the ages into your muscles. You let the body dictate what's going to happen, and you let the body dictate this in its own time rather than, say, to a measured beat of four. You learn that a certain motion takes a certain amount of time, followed by a little choppy time. And uses of energy, uses of dynamics. How a thing is supposed to be done, rather than *what* is being done. How it is to be done.

In improvisation you hold yourself in readiness. Your instrument —your body—is trained; then you begin to find out about *it*, its potential for movement in every body part. The arm can move certain ways, the head can move certain ways, the spine can move certain ways. How do they all fit together? What are their potentials? What are their expressive values in general? In class we start with specific problems: do an improvisation that shows me your arm and particularly your elbow. Show me your elbow.

By isolating one little part of the body the dancer is forced to lend all his concentration to it. He begins to find out, with all his concentration focused, what is possible with that one point of the body. You can explore all areas—spatial areas, shape areas, motional and energy areas—whatever is possible, as long as your whole body and your whole psyche are tuned into this one area.

How do you do this?

You have to practice a lot. You must have a teacher skilled in improvisation who can tell you when it's happening and when it's not. Actually you know, but it's a shortcut to have the teacher say, "This is when it was happening, and this is when it was not happening."

Can you feel it?

You can feel it happening, particularly when you're improvising with someone else. Suddenly something takes over and you are lending yourself to the larger experience rather than simply controlling what is happening. It's not that you lose control. It's that you are a willing participant in an action larger than yourself. Even when you're improvising by yourself that can happen, but more rarely. It's easier with a partner because there is another element, another body to contend with. Therefore the action, the event is larger than what just you have control of, and you have to open yourself up to the other body's impulses as well as your own.

Improvisation training has to include interaction with other people, other bodies as well, so that you depend not only on the same old mannerisms coming out of your body, but also on someone else's messages coming across the space to you. You have to respond to that, so you are made larger by the fact that your concentration is pulled out of your body, out into the space, out to other people, other bodies around you.

This is all in preparation (in Murray's thought anyway) for the moment of performance. If you are then large enough psychically and physically to go on the stage and be ready to interact with others around you, with the music, costumes, lighting, sound, whatever is important in the piece that you are involved in, your expressive effect on an audience is made that much greater. If you go on stage feeling self-conscious, thinking you're wearing an unattractive costume or your knee hurts or you have a hangover and everything is going wrong today, you can't possibly become a part of the happening. Murray encourages the improvisation training specifically for this moment on stage—for the art moment.

Our improvisational training is the thing that gives us the skill to recognize and to fulfill the motional aspect of what we do, because improvisation is concerned with the absolutely spontaneous moment— the now. It's a learned skill to be able to pick up and amplify the thing that is existing.

"Improvisation" is such a catchall word; different people mean different things by it. It's very interesting to sit in during Murray's lecture/demonstrations because no one in the audience ever believes that you're actually improvising.

Those lecture/demonstrations are a special case, because we do the same one everywhere; that is, the structure is consistent. We always include body parts, space and shape, and sometimes we demonstrate time. But of course the improvisations themselves are really improvised, the dancing is different. However, the set—where you put your mind when you begin—is the same every time you start. The people who feed in and feed out may be in a different order, and you may be dancing with someone different each time, but the area of concentration in each section of the demonstration is the same; to show body parts; to show shape; to show space. We acquire an ease of slipping into these mind sets so that what we do becomes polished and sophisticated. It's not that we know what we're going to do but that we all agree on a certain area of endeavor which makes it cohesive for the audience.

Another thing about lecture/demonstrations is that we are doing a kind of improvisation that is not taught. We are doing improvisation as illustration, not for our own personal exploration. In class you are always improvising for your own growth and exploration. Never are you called upon to consider that you're doing this for an audience—unless perhaps you are doing a shape improvisation, and you have to present the best face toward the audience, rather than turn your back and make all the shapes upstage where no one can see them. Maybe that's one exception. But in class you're not asked to *show* space or the body part, you're asked to feel it yourself. There's a vast difference. Sometimes when I teach the advanced class at the school I ask them to do performing improvisations rather than felt improvisations.

Our company has this sort of skewed presentational idea when we show the improvisations in lecture/demonstrations. It is for an audience, and it is to illustrate an idea rather than to explore for ourselves. Also we have the advantage that we have worked within the same ideas for so long that we have a lot of common ground to work on so that things become clear for an audience. We don't have to find ourselves. We can almost immediately show what we want to show. That's our job. Performed improvisation is very good because it makes us edit out the ambiguities and forces us into clarity. In our lecture/demonstrations we find that simple things, even though they may seem boring to us sometimes, are startlingly clear to the audience and make the audience see what has been talked about.

Thus in performance we can go through a choreographed piece in our minds and say, "All right, in this piece I can afford to be as complex in my inner or outer spatial play as I want to be because I am the focus of what's going on." Or, in a large unison section you have to cool it and make your choices of transition or timing simple and in accord with the group. Otherwise there gets to be too much to see; the eye blurs rather than focusing clearly on what is happening. I think in Murray's choreography the concern is that the audience's eye be directed to one part of the stage or the other to give a narrative: look upstage left because there's a little duet happening there. The rest of the people on stage are fairly quiet or even directing their attention to that corner so that the audience also watches it. When that's finished or has run a certain course, the rest of the stage opens out and becomes more active. The performers know when to cool it and when to belt it. Improvisation training is invaluable for that.

I don't know in how many other techniques we would be discussing improvisation in relation to performance. I think it is central to Murray's technique, but I'm not sure how necessary it is to others.

Improvisation, as I got it in college, or as I'm told it is being offered around the country, is taught as an adjunct. At the University of Utah it was called "Composition 2." The idea of improvisation was as an igniter to creation, to choreography, as a place to find ideas for dances. I think that's the majority opinion of its usefulness. By freeing yourself from preconceived steps, by letting spontaneity take over, you will find new ground, new reference points to dance about or create works about, even new steps. We get asked that a lot around the country as we do our lecture/demonstrations. They ask Murray if he uses his dancers' improvisations, and he says that's not what it is for in our technique. But that seems to be almost a universal idea of what it is.

That's why I wanted to discuss it.

It's usually considered a place where seeds are planted and a place where the seeds of new choreography come from. That's perfectly valid, I suppose, if the choreographer or the person directing the improvisation has the eye to pick out the things that are needed or things that touch him or her and that could be expanded upon and turned into dances. That's a completely valid method of mining choreographic pay dirt. But I think the choreographer then has to be extremely self-disciplined about what to keep and what to throw out because a lot of stuff coming out of improvisation can be very seductive but have nothing to do with the piece he wants to do. Some people conduct guided improvisations, or they have a very loose structure which they feed to the dancers first, and the dancers follow the very loose structure and they call that a finished piece. They even make an evening of that and call it a performance, which, I suppose is another way of making dances.

But unless the dancers are extremely skilled (and so rarely are they) it's unfair to make the audience sit through the exploration, through the garbage in order to find the diamonds. The diamonds are there.

I suppose anyone who opens himself up can find wonderful materials in improvisation. But if you want to keep the audience in mind—if you're not doing it just for yourself—then I think you have to be the editor. You have to be selective about what you put in front of an audience. I myself would never be tempted to put on a directed improvisation for an audience—unless I had the Murray Louis Dance Company, which is so skilled.

We actually did that one evening—in Minneapolis, and it was smashingly successful. We worked in tandem with an opera company which was improvising vocally while we were improvising dancing, and it was stunning because we had very good people. Very risky, very risky. It could fall flat on its face even with sophisticated, good dancers. If things don't click in a certain way it could become erratic and improbable. If you can keep yourself concentrated, you have a good chance. But that's a big if. I wouldn't want to chance it with most dancers.

But as far as all of you are concerned, improvisation leads into something else.

Oh yes. It serves as a way of sensitizing our instruments—our minds and our bodies—so that we can bring all our nerve endings to a performance and have all our signals flashing at once, rather than be asleep in the head while the body does the movement and the psyche shrinks into itself. It makes a difference on stage. The audience may not be as aware of it as fellow dancers would be. If you pull any part of yourself back it detracts from the performance. I'm speaking from a vantage point of experience, so that I know when all the stops are out and when something is being pulled back. Recently in Florida I was performing with a very stiff back and it was depressing to me because I knew I couldn't depend on my body to answer all the signals coming in to me and I couldn't depend on it to send out everything I wanted to, just as I wanted to, because there was a stiffness. That's a physical block—you can also have a mental block or emotional block—and it was depressing to me because I knew that I was not a clear channel. It was not good for me. An audience may not be at all aware of something like that, but may get a little itchy. I get a little itchy when I see that on stage. I can watch performers and say "head problems," or "that back won't bend" or "it looks like she had a rough night," but an ordinary audience wouldn't see that so much.

So your improvisation training helps to make each performance live?

Yes. You can say a dance performance is just directing energies, and the audience is taking in the energy that's coming from the stage. Patterns of energy are happening on the stage, and if the dancers who are the motors, the generators, are not generating, the audience is confused because it doesn't know what to watch. If the dancer *is* energized, *is* generating in a predetermined direction the audience is not confused. You have to believe that the audience is innocent and must be shown where to look, how to look, what to see. If you go by rote through your performance there's no way that you can make the energy live through you.

   If you're alone on the stage and if you are a very experienced performer, you can get through on muscle memory by doing steps beautifully. But if you are not charged to the level that the piece demands, the warp and the woof are not complete, a hole shows in the choreography and the audience is restless.

   In so much dance there are more holes than warp and woof. Perhaps star performances are supposed to carry the piece, or music is, or the intellectual thread is. You can see what the choreographer meant to do and you can see the shell of it. But that to me is an intellectual appreciation I would rather forego. I would like to have it hit me a little lower rather than just through the eye and the brain.

   That is the communicative value of motion. That's the thing that comes across to the audience unless they are just sitting there watching with their minds saying, "Oh yes, I see what the choreographer meant by that," which I'm afraid is the way most dance watching is accomplished. We would rather the intent be perceived through the muscles and the tendons and the guts of what's being done.

How does this work in a specific dance?

In performance you have the structure of the movement, the general thrust and intent of the piece. You know the large line structure of it because you have the music or you have a series of movements that take an amount of time to accomplish. Then the training in improvisation comes in and you become attuned to the larger thing. It's more than just what you are doing at the moment, you realize that there is a span which has to be accomplished, which has to be shown.

You begin *Porcelain Dialogues* very informally; you're sitting with your back to the audience. The first thing that happens is you turn around. Everyone looks at Robert Small and Robert stands up, walks around and looks at everyone, then walks downstage and begins "the dancing." But the thing is that the dancing started when the curtain opened. The audience may not realize that, but the dancer has to know it. That opening tableau, with all the backs to the audience, is a strong opening statement of—well, you don't know what until later on, when finally, something has been accomplished. The opening is the clue, and the turning around all at once is a bigger clue. As an individual performer you're aware that this overall thing has to be accomplished.

Murray, in his choreography, allows you a lot of latitude in a time sense—particularly in *Porcelain Dialogues* [choreographed in three sections to two movements of the Tchaikovsky Quartet in D] which is not danced beat to beat except in the second section. In the first section it is choreographed in great chunks, sometimes approximately with the music, sometimes not. But you know, roughly, when you're supposed to end, according to the music. Most often, particularly in the first section anyway, you cue off the other dancers. When they're finished, you begin. That's what has to happen in *Porcelain Dialogues.* In a dialogue one person speaks and the other replies. The process goes on until a whole statement has been spoken.

The improvisation comes in the timing between the steps, the dance movements. Murray always says that he leaves the transitions between the steps up to us.

Michael illustrates a movement in a run-through of *Glances.* (*top, l. to r.:* Michael, Helen, Sara, Bill, Robert, Murray; *bottom, l. to r.:* Michael, Helen, Sara, Bill, Murray, Robert)

Could you explain exactly what you mean by transitions?

Transitions are what happen *between* dance movements. They are the subtle nuances—the transitional material—between the steps. For example, the arm makes a large circle in space twice, then the feet have a short run across the stage, then the whole body bends over, hands touching the floor. Now, that's three elements. There's the two big circles with the arms, the short run across the stage, and the bending over till the hands touch the floor. Those are the three gross movements.

In between, there is a change from the end of the second arm circle to the run, then there's another at the end of the run. When does the run stop? Where does it stop? How does that run stop in order to enable the body to bend over, hands finally touching the floor, which is the accomplishment of the phrase. The dancer has to find the right amount of energy to accomplish each thing within the line structure that he's been given.

The timing will change from performance to performance because first of all the dancer is a different person from performance to performance. Every day is different. You feel lazy and slow one day and the next day you're absolutely on top of it and you're bubbling around. The performance will show that. Your decision as to how you'll get from one thing to the next is governed by your own chemistry, by your own mood.

One of the advantages of performing a lot is that you know how you feel before the show. I went through about four years of performing before I even realized that I was in different states of mind before the curtain went up. Now, I think, how could I ever be so dumb as not to realize that there are other things going on all the time inside you? But I do remember at the time, when I was in that sort of limbo, Phyllis Lamhut would say, "I have to pull myself down to get ready for the show. I have to pull my scattered energies together so that I can deliver at a certain level." Other times you have to dredge yourself up from all your aches and pains and say, I have to get up to this level, or I have to get down, or I have to pull in, or I have to let out. All these things you have to know. Young dancers have to do it instinctively because they don't know any better. They have to live long enough to find out about themselves. I like it, now, because I can tell about myself and how I feel, so I have some clue before the curtain goes up as to what's going to happen and what I have to do. I suppose that's what maturity in a performer is: knowing beforehand. It's not a big surprise when the curtain goes up.

What about responding to other people's transitions?

Okay. Let's say you have come into the performance, at a certain level of nervous intensity. Suddenly someone dashes at you from across the stage. You have to be able to absorb what they've knocked you over with, and pull it down to the professional level of delivery. Or a timing thing will throw you. The other night Tony Miccoci, the stage manager, took his time about making a slide change which we were depending on for a movement cue, and we all got nervous. At that moment all we could do was look across the stage at each other and send the question silently: What are we going to do now? As it happened we broke into the next movement almost simultaneously, I think before we got the visual cue from the slides. That is when your training is invaluable. When you're on stage you have a level to deliver and you have to absorb all the energies coming around you and deliver at that level and have your own energies under enough control.

In every piece.

Absolutely, and in *Personnae* even more, because *Personnae* is so very free. There is not a single count, there is not even a music cue in the first movement, which is a good four minutes long. There's not a single music cue in it to tell you, is the music about over? Am I in the right place at the right time? You can get your cue only from the other dancers, so timing is everything. You have to be attentive; you can never rest. I don't suppose I ever go on stage now with my psychic level at rest because I know it doesn't work. I know I have gone on stage that way, and perhaps I had a minor enough role to get away with it. At least in the sense of not committing any great faux pas on stage. Still, when your psychic level is not up you disappear. No one notices you. No one sees you onstage. Or, if everyone else is up and you are not, every eye goes to you and says, why am I disturbed by that person's presence on stage?

Murray is emphatic in insisting that we be on top of what we're doing. In pieces like *Proximities* and *Porcelain Dialogues*, which have romantic scores, it is easy to sit on the music—particularly in something like the second movement of *Porcelain Dialogues*, which is

counted and danced on the beat and has a lovely melody that
everyone knows and recognizes. It is easy to say, "I can float along on
this, I can follow the music, do the movement, and everything will
come out fine," because you know there are no decisions about how
long to take, how much energy to give.

Murray is infuriated with that kind of dancing because it's
passive. The structure of the dance is still there but he will not settle
for structure without communicative value. The steps are not the
communication for Murray. They're like the flour in the cake recipe—
the first thing that's there. Within the movement are all the
considerations of space, time, use of energy, and, beyond that,
emotional or poetic implications which as a performer you don't
necessarily have to have in your head all the time, depending on the
piece. But you must be aware of all the physical and dynamic things
that are going into what you're doing. If you simply do the steps you
might as well be in a marching band or be doing Rockette routines,
which rely on precision to satisfy the eye. You can do those dances
precisely, and they'll be as dull as dishwater.

And they'll be the same every night.

And they won't be worth seeing. That's why in spectacle dance, in
ballet and certain aspects of modern dance, you go time after time to
see great performers, to see what a new artist can do with the same
old role, because they lend their individuality to what has gone before.
You can go to the American Ballet Theater's *Swan Lake;* they have
six or seven women who do the ballerina role, and you can derive
satisfaction from the truth that happens through their bodies. It's
certainly not the steps you go for. You've seen the steps, and to see
the steps again, even executed beautifully, is pointless, because, after a
while, simple precision wears thin. If it's a heavily dramatic role you
see the passion. And always, always you are more interested in the
how than in the what. How does she achieve her effect? How does
she get across her intention?

This is what Murray demands of us. We always must know the
how of what we are doing. We cannot be satisfied with just doing the
what, we have to do the *how* as well. And we have to do it
consciously. We can rely greatly on intuition and on spontaneity, but
we have to know that we have those resources available to us. You
achieve your basic level by knowing how a thing is gotten at, not

what it is. Any third-year dance student can do the steps, and any third-year dance student who has a great deal of stretch and a great deal of poise can do the movement beautifully. That's not what Murray is interested in and that's not what Nikolais is interested in. Great dancers will deliver the steps at a professional level and then go beyond that for their own satisfaction, because that's what their endeavor is about. They conquer the physical routine and go beyond in order to get to the deeper, more universal truth. Connecting to humanity rather than to a machine precision.

That's why the audience keeps coming back.

Yes, precisely.

The how includes all the other things? Like the transitions?

Right, and the awareness of space, time, energy. Another word for "how" is quality. That's what it means: quality, and qualities of movement.

I want to talk about nuance.

In performance the nuance of energy that we work with, the spontaneity of reaction, the very small, subtle kinds of action and reaction and movements between the steps—the transitional material —all this makes an atmosphere. It's like the water that a fish is in. It's there, but the fish is not particularly aware of it. Just so, the audience is not aware of the atmosphere, except for knowing that the dancers are agreed upon what is happening, that the dancers are of one mind about the presentation of the piece. And that must be comforting to an audience because if there's a schizophrenia on stage, the audience gets confused and a little puzzled. A lot of dance concerts I go to puzzle me, particularly if the dancers are presenting the material as if it meant something, or there is some obvious symbolism which you feel you're missing out on as you sit there and watch. I think our work does not have that kind of symbolism, or at least not intentionally. Maybe Murray puts it in the choreography and the structure and we don't even suspect it's there. We do it as structure rather than as the underlying thing, as the nuance.

Could you use the word "vision" instead of "atmosphere?"

No, the vision is Murray's. He has created the conditions that we perform in. He expects us to lend the nuance or to lend ourselves to the evocation of what he wants to say so that his vision is enhanced by our individual peculiarities, coming out of us but through a common channel. The dancers are in agreement through a common feeling, a common atmosphere.

Murray tells us what he wants. He may not tell us his vision. For example, in this new piece he's choreographing [*Glances*, premiered at the Connecticut College American Dance Festival, August 1976] he's not talking, he's just giving us the steps, which is all right. I have a feeling that after it's choreographed and after we have a score for it we'll begin to suspect a little bit more what it's about, but it's very abstract. It's also technically difficult. So it's enough to concern ourselves with the steps for now. Once the steps are down pat we can start thinking a bit more about nuance, I suppose. There's going to be lots of nuance because each section has a totally different character from all the others. It's going to be an interesting piece.

What's it called?

It has no title, nothing. He hasn't given one word. He let spill to someone and it got back to me that he was going to make it a difficult technical piece and that's what it is.

Talk about your solo in Geometrics.

Geometrics was composed as an abstract piece. We knew from the beginning that it was going to be called something like "geometrics" or "patterns." It was obvious from the beginning that he was working with patterns—spatial patterns, stage patterns. He got through one or two or three sections and then said, "All right, I want to work with Michael now." So we went into the room and he just started on steps. He started with the squatting and the swaying on the floor and he didn't give me any indication of what it was about or any feeling about it. He just gave me the steps. The only indication I got of what he wanted was that at one point there's a spectacle kind of leaping. He would give it to me and watch me do it and say, "Is there a way that would look higher or better or more spectacular?" We worked on that for a while, and it was very tiring. But as for meaning or nuance or anything like that, nothing. There was no indication of what the solo was about, and it turned into a long solo. It's two and a half minutes long, or something like that.

I like it because it's about something else every time I see it.

Well, that reflects on me because I performed it for a year before I decided this thing must be about something. Right at the beginning I had said, half jokingly: this is a dance about a frog who dreams of being a prince. It was something to go on, because the solo starts low on the floor, I stand up and do some things, and then it ends low again. I thought: it's anchored, then it breaks out, then it goes back to its anchor again. So what does that mean? And still I don't find a dramatic line in it. There are dramatic moments, which I tend to play up because I have a bent toward dramatic expression anyway—strange, for someone in such an abstractly oriented company—but every time I'm left to my own devices I tend to get dramatic.

Anyway I was left to my own devices in the solo. Murray has said nothing about it. Well, he never sees it, he's backstage, and from the side a dance always looks different anyway, so it's hard to say anything.

Recently he cut a lot of *Geometrics*. He snipped out pieces that didn't necessarily have to be there, and he cut out a chunk of my solo, which was all right because it was too long.

When?

It was last fall sometime, I think. This last season at NYU [New York University] it was shorter than the version you saw before. It was at the same time that he cut the girls' dance out of it. The girls had a big quartet which was dropped. At the same time he cut my solo, he cut Robert's solo, and now he's talking about adding a new finale to *Geometrics* or rechoreographing the ending of it.

He never gave me an image, he never gave me a dramatic line, and I couldn't find one. So I thought that all I could do then was to attack this as I've been trained to do, and that was to do the steps and modulate the transitions with as much skill as I could. That's all I've been able to do with it—work on the transitions and the timing. There is too much music for the length of dancing I have now so I have lots of time to play around and do holds. But I'm worried that if I stop too long in those high poses with my arm up, does the energy line of the piece stop also? Or is there some way that I can stand there and keep the energy line moving while I'm not moving? Can the energy line move while I stand still? Things like that concern me now. Mainly timing. I think that's been my thing. I play with the timing from performance to performance, and it's always different. Some people hate the whole thing, and other people say it's really a fine solo.

I love it. It's mysterious and it stays in your mind and you wonder all kinds of things about it.

Do you want to know the real reason that solo is there and that it's the way it is? I think it's because Murray had three parts preceeding it which were real motion pieces. A lot of stuff was going on and he needed a place where things quieted down. One person is on stage, there isn't a whole lot of movement; the audience gets to rest their eye. That's a terrible burden to put on one person. Now is the time for you folks to sit back and rest a bit. And yet there has to be something there that is being carried through. So it's up to me to provide a breather and yet be intriguing.

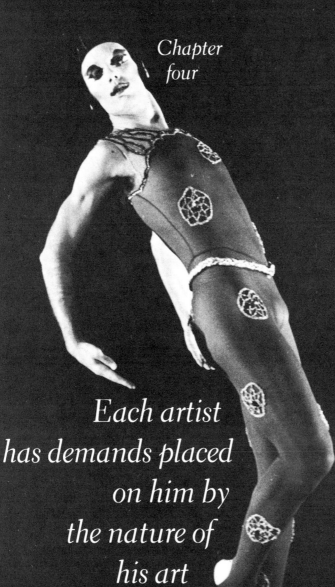

Each artist
has demands placed
on him by
the nature of
his art

The Body
Warm-up
Dance Captain
Performance
Theaters and Audiences
The Ego

The next conversation took place in Mill River, Massachusetts, after the Murray Louis Dance Company's appearance at The Jacob's Pillow Dance Festival. It was the beginning of a three-week vacation for the company. We sat outside under a pine tree and talked.

Let's talk about caring for the body. If you're a dancer what kind of things do you think about that ordinary mortals don't?

First of all, the instrument of the dancer is his body, much as the instrument of the musician is his cello or his piano. The great difference is that we not only play our instrument, we also live in our instrument, and that creates problems. You can put a Stradivarius in a case and keep it away from heat and moisture. You can't do this with your body. Yet it is subject to all conditions of humidity, light, and heat as well as poor food and good food, and so the dancer seems to outside observers to be obsessed with his body. Whenever dancers get together there's body talk, endless body talk. Outsiders are bored or amazed or tolerant of this body talk. But it's of the essence to dancers because if their bodies are not in peak condition they are not operating optimally in their chosen field of endeavor. A dancer's body demands so much attention; you can't relax. In a period of performance you are always considering, if I relax this much am I relaxing too much? Or not enough? Am I eating all the right things? Am I getting enough sleep? These things should concern everyone, of course. But the human body is resilient enough so that the average person can give a little, store up abuses and then lavish care on it later, during vacations.

But dancers can't do that. They have to be constantly primed for their professional action, which is dancing. If the body is not highly tuned they're not earning their keep because they're not delivering the way they're supposed to. So their bodies have to be kept at peak level all the time, and this gets to be a real drag because the human body and the human emotional system don't want to do that. It seems to be an unnatural way of living because ups and downs are natural. You want to have periods of great work followed by periods of great rest. The whole human being is, I think, fulfilled by that kind of a cycle more than by having to stay at optimum performing pitch for nine weeks on tour. After those nine weeks the body is really ready to let down for a couple of weeks. But you can't let it go beyond a couple of weeks because the muscles begin to tighten up, the joints begin to grinch, the back begins to spasm, and you know you've got to get back into shape or you're going to fall apart. The fact is that you aren't going to fall apart, but you're letting yourself in for a great deal of pain during the process of getting yourself back in shape.

So you learn not to get too far out of shape even in your relaxation periods.

Exactly. This is the first of three weeks off for us. At a time like this I am willing to go two weeks without moving. After that I like to take some ballet lessons, which work my body in a different way and do not tax me. The particular ballet classes I take give me exercise without making me go too far. In other words, just to get the blood moving through the muscles is the important thing. For me. I certainly wouldn't want dance students to have that kind of attitude toward dance classes. They are always working to perfect and to hone themselves toward the perfection of the body as far as any individual body can be perfected.

How long does it take before you become fully aware of your own body, its capacities and its likes and dislikes?

In *A Dancer's World* Martha Graham says it takes ten years before a dancer is able to trust his body to do what he commands it to do. I

agree that it takes ten years to make a mature performer. Murray says
he can make a professional dancer in three years, but that assumes a
great deal.

*That's interesting. When I went down to Henry Street in June of 1970,
Murray was saying that it took ten years to make a dancer.*

Right. He's changed his ideas. He says three years now because he's
seen it happen in three years, I think. If you have someone like
Robert Small. His body is proportionally very good. His mind is prone
to the type of concentration that's demanded of a dancer. When we
first saw him as a student we were astounded at his ability to
concentrate on what he was doing. If you have these things going for
you, you have a head start. That's the kind of person you can turn
into a professional dancer in three years. By "professional" I mean
someone who can deliver at a certain minimum level consistently.
That's what a professional dancer is. I felt myself reaching maturity
only after about ten years of dance.

Does that mean from your first dance class?

Yes. I started to feel the rich reverberations happening after ten years.
The first five of those years were student years, with great chunks of
summer layovers when nothing happened. Then four, four and a half
years of professional dancing happened. Good hard performing
happened before I started to feel my maturity coming on. About the
time I was thirty I started to feel really on top of things. Now I'm
thirty-three, and so I've had three years of that. But I feel myself
constantly growing, constantly more aware of my physical being
because it's more demanding. The more in shape you are, the less
choice you have in the way you treat your body. It demands certain
things. It demands a certain amount of exercise, a certain amount of
food, a certain amount of sleep, and so on.

And you have to accede to those demands.

You have to accede or you fall apart. Because you are placing certain
demands on your body, it in turn demands great care.

*Do these things get passed down? Were you taught what to do or did
you just learn?*

People can tell you these things over and over, and it never sinks in until one day your back is in spasm and there are things you have to do to work it out, maybe vitamins you have to take, diet, sleep and so on.

How do you find out these things, though?

It's just experience. A little thing happens, then another, and it grows. It becomes a volume of experience which becomes a condition of life. You condition your existence to these physical demands which are placed upon you by your organism, by your instrument.

While we were performing at Jacob's Pillow, at the hotel we were staying at was a professional flutist who practiced four hours a day. That was his discipline. On his own he was working on his double tonguing—takka-takka-takka-takka—trying to get it faster and faster. He had a metronome in his practice room, and he did it and did it. We were all grateful that he was as good and as proficient as he was, and that he played Bach and Ravel, which were nice to hear.

So each artist has demands placed upon him by the nature of his art, and the nature of our art is first of all physical, because of the instrument. Later on other demands make themselves felt. You have to achieve a certain stability in your own emotional, intellectual life. This all goes into your maturity. In your youth you don't have to have any of that. You can just go out there and knock it out, which is the nice thing.

Right now, for example, my back is giving me problems because my spine is achieving new degrees of suppleness which it hasn't had.

What is happening?

Well, my spine is bothering me in two places. One is at the very base, almost into the pelvic structure. There's a whole series of vertebrae that are not used to moving against each other, they're just used to holding rigid and holding the body up. There are muscles between them, and when you start to stretch those muscles and pull the vertebrae apart, lengthening yourself out, stretching in ways you are not used to, those muscles say no. They go into spasm, and you have to work them out and coax them into becoming more supple than they're used to being.

The other problem is toward the middle of my back, between my shoulder blades. The arms are attached by muscles to the shoulder

blades, which are attached by muscles to the vertebrae. That's a very
strong point of tension because all the arm work comes out of that
place in the vertebrae, and you are taught—particularly in our
technique—to work your arms from way deep in the back. And so
when I get back to the city I'm going to a chiropractor and have him
work on it. But that will be the first time I've sought professional help
for any of my aches and pains. Other dancers are constantly at the
doctors or the chiropractors or god knows what else, to try to work
out their problems.

The human spine was not constructed to work vertically, it was
constructed to work horizontally, and standing vertically puts a great
load on it which it was not meant to bear structurally. The lower part
of the spine from the middle of the back down curves in toward the
body and then curves out again as it comes down into the pelvic
structure. Everybody has that. The vertebrae are set one on top of
another, they have a certain amount of elasticity one way or the other
from side to side, and they're attached to each other by muscles and
the stuff that holds you up. From about the waistline down into the
pelvis there's a goodly number of vertebrae clear down into a little
tailbone. In most people the vertebrae are just held in one position
because that's all you need in order to walk or run or carry on your
daily life. Your pelvic structure is held in one slant all the time, while
the legs move out of that. That's enough for most people. But the
dancer has to have a greater range of possibilities, because the hip is
the way station for all the energy impulses from the top down to the
legs and from the ground through the legs up through the hip into
the spine. Some dance techniques call for very rigidly held buttock
muscles that stop the energy flow right there where the hips are
locked. If the energy is frozen there, you have less possibility of
nuance up and down your body.

Now, in order to get more suppleness in there we have a series
of exercises that stretch out the muscles in the back—exercises for
bending over and rounding forward. Consequently the part of the
back which is used to curving inward is flattened out or even pushed
the other way toward the outside. This doesn't do any physiological
damage to the spine, but the muscles are not used to moving that
way and they protest.

In my case I've gone through a certain series of those exercises
and the muscles have done their protesting and it's over with. Well,

now I've gotten way down into the very bottom vertebrae, which never move at all in most people. In a lot of people, after a time they fuse together, the vertebrae are solid, and it's all right because most people don't need to use them.

For me, those down there are moving now. They are attached to many small muscles and muscles that are important in posture and in holding the structure up. Every time I stand up they are grinched one way, and when I lie down they relax and another set takes over, and then when I'm dancing they are all stretching. And they protest. When I'm standing up they hurt one way, when I lie down they hurt another way, when I'm on my side they hurt yet another way. It's a drag.

How do you get them not to hurt?

Warm-up. Warm-up makes them feel much better. I do back exercises morning and evening that help a great deal, that eases them. I'm just hoping that after a time of being loose they'll become accustomed to being loose and won't hurt so much.

That happened to you because you got deeper and deeper into using those muscles. Did you do that consciously?

Yes, sure. It was the result of our stretches—the way we are trained. I'm changing the tilt of my hip a little bit forward. If you ran a line down the middle of the pelvis it would tilt from somewhere in front of the chest until it hit the ground someplace behind the feet. I'm trying to change the tilt so that the center line of the hip is straight up and down through the body, and that involves a lot of stretching along the front of the hip too. This vertical setup is more practical for dancing, because it places your weight more immediately at your disposal in all directions. Your hips are pressed forward, your weight is on the balls of your feet rather than back on your heels, and that makes you able to move in any direction quickly like a boxer or a fencer. It's more efficient and it frees other things in your hip joint to work more easily.

What about your shoulders?

That's another story. I have spasms between my shoulder blades. Not spasms any more; it just gets tight and hurts.

What caused this?

There is a section in *Proximities* where the boys line up and the girls
jump on them and then the boys pass the girls over. I take each of
the girls, place her feet on my right thigh (I'm squatting kind of low),
and pick her up with my arms and over my chest. Then I lift her up
and set her feet down on my other thigh. Then she stands up and
falls over onto the next person. Well, that lifting, pressing to my
chest, and lifting up and over with my arms and chest put all the
weight on one spot in my spine—three people every time we did
Proximities, and we've done it a lot. I think it probably pinched the
nerves and muscles and maybe even deteriorated the bone slightly.
But also I used to be able to crack my back right there, by pressing
on the front of my ribs and getting into a certain position. I could
make a pop happen there, and I can't do that any more. I have a
feeling that I made it too loose with the popping and then put too
much pressure there when I was dancing in *Proximities.* I just had a
bad combination, and now I have to live with the consequences.
We've staged *Proximities* so that I'm not in that position in the line
any more. Robert has to take over that part. We've traded places in
that one little section, and Murray said it looked all right so there was
no problem.

   That's the story of my shoulders. They tense up at night when I
sleep and when I don't use the muscles. The lower spine is curious; it
has its own life. This morning I had no pain in my lower spine when
I woke up, which is unusual, and very little in the middle. It depends
probably on psychic health too. You can be released and relaxed in
your mind, and your muscles relax too. So often your problems are
psychosomatic.

Even visible ones?

Oh yes. A lot of dancers are injured because they are not happy with
what they are doing and they get careless. In Nikolais's company
there was a rash of injuries during a particularly unhappy time in the
company. The mind takes over. The mind says: if this situation is
intolerable there are ways to get out of it. And one of those ways is
taken, whether as a conscious decision of the dancer or not. Of course
there is the legitimate accident where someone kicks your foot out

from under you just as your weight is going onto it, but I would say that eighty percent of onstage accidents are caused by the person's own mental condition.

Let's return to warm-up. Would you explain it further?

In the general philosophy behind our warm-up the first thing is that we try to warm up all parts of the body so that they are ready to move. The second thing is that we try to stretch the muscles to give them greater range of movement so that they can do larger things, more stageworthy rather than pedestrian things. The third thing is to do all those things with a minimum of tension, particularly since we do the same thing over and over every day. I think students who take stretches with the company are a little dismayed at the very lax discipline in our warm-up, and we may be unique in that sense because we do things very informally. If I don't feel like doing a certain exercise on a certain day I can go off and do my own variation, or work on another kind of thing which I feel is more important at the time.

We begin with the spine. The spine is really the most complex joint/muscle configuration in the body because there are so many different little bones and so many different little muscles. We work by rounding it out, straightening it out, doing bounces, release and recovery, which works the muscles gently. Gets the blood into the muscles, which is always advantageous because the blood carries oxygen to the muscles and carries away the waste which the muscles produce all the time. That's what muscle soreness is—a great buildup of waste in the muscles. So you try to get the blood in there to carry away the waste.

After we do the back we get into the legs and the hip joints, particularly the hip joints, another great source of concern. The hip joints are constructed in a way which allows them to move freely in certain directions. But the muscles around them tend to tighten up quickly and the muscles that are in the hip joint moving into the thighs can freeze quickly, so we try to lengthen those out, stretch them out early in the warmup. We flex and reach the legs in a number of ways which work all the muscles gently. Later on we get into more serious stretching after they're warmed up a bit, because to stretch them when they're cold is to invite spasm and pulling of the tendons and the muscles.

Then we go into whole variations of spine and leg work and we even do some push-ups for the arms.

Why push-ups?

Why push-ups? Well, the men have to lift the women now and again. They always say that in lifting, at least half the work is done by the women. So the women do it too, as much as they can and as much as they want to. It's not required. Some of them just lie there during the warm-ups. I can't blame them.

And so the hour of stretching and warming up is a general progression all over the body, getting things moving. After forty-five minutes or so, we stand up and do pliés, the classic exercise of any dancer. Ballet classes begin with pliés. But we don't do them as a limbering-up exercise. We do them as an exercise in spatial awareness. Going into our lower space, coming up out of it into a higher space and going down, going up and standing in second position with the feet wide and the arms wide, going out into width and up into height —we work it spatially that way. That's a revelation to dancers who don't come from our technique. They don't understand because they've done a million pliés, just bending the knees and straightening them. That's what they understand as pliés—kneebends.

Pliés are to us the quintessential dance exercise because they are not only working the muscles, they're working your mind as well, developing your energy flow, from one part of the body to the other, to the space around you. Holding your arms in the ballet fifth position front, which is rounded arms in front of you, we encompass a volume with our arms. In ballet you see the rounded arms as the important thing. For us it is the rounded space in front of us which the arms encompass. We become aware of that. Also when we stand up we become aware of our chests because the top part of the sternum is actually the escape point from the body for a great deal of energy directions. The energy we have found seems to originate in the solar plexus. In other words, Isadora Duncan was right when she said all of dance originated in the solar plexus. And Martha Graham got at that also with her contractions. And Merce Cunningham says the spine, which is very close.

The energy originates in the solar plexus, is lifted up into the chest, and for us is a great deal of the time emanated through the top part of the sternum. The projection, what is called stage projection, for us happens through the top part of the sternum. That's one of our secrets. That's why when Nikolais-Louis dancers stand on the stage they aren't rigidly presenting the human form. They are standing there with an energy flow coming up and out through the sternum. And as you move forward the sternum pulls you forward across the stage. If you are to go backward, you drop some of that sternum forwardness and go back into your lower spine, because your center of gravity is down there.

That's why you all walk so beautifully.

Yes, and actually it's scientifically a very efficient way to walk. The machine, the instrument, the body is set up so that if you are walking forward as if being pulled by a string from the sternum, you are using the muscle and the structure of your body most efficiently. And also you are most ready to change direction quickly. As you walk forward with your sternum the forwardmost part of your body, you are stepping on the front part of your foot rather than the heel. The pedestrian walk is heel-toe, heel-toe. We step forward and land on the front part of our foot first.

Boxers, fencers, basketball players move on the balls of their feet. It makes them ready to change direction quickly. Dancers need the same thing. Ballet dancers place a greater emphasis on the end of the toe hitting the floor first. For us that's too great an emphasis on foot technique, whereas the ball is actually what receives the weight rather than the ends of the toes. If you have that split second of toe-ball, toe-ball, you are making a fractional time loss as you take your step, whereas if you step on the ball of your foot, the foot receives the weight instantly.

Ballet dancers criticize us for not pointing our toes a lot of the time, not "completing the line," because we are using the ball of the foot as the furthest extension of the leg and the toes are cushioning, qualifying instruments for receiving the weight. That's the scientific explanation. It gives our movement a softer attack, particularly walking and running across the stage. It gives a softer look to the legs. A lot of dancers prefer a very hard-edged use of the leg because a hard edge is more spectacular. It punches the image into the eye

In rehearsal for the solo from *Geometrics.* (Michael

more emphatically when you're using extreme stretching out of the leg clear to the ends of the toes. Now, we also use the stretched toe and the stretched leg to indicate spatial concerns, because the energy flowing along the leg out of the toes will extend the toes very strongly. But I don't do much of that any more. In the warm-up exercises, when I really extend my toes fully I cramp, and I wouldn't if I were used to extending it that way strongly, so I find that my foot extension is through an extended ball of the foot with the toes released, which gives a softer look. It is not as linear a look as a ballet dancer achieves by a full extension.

After we've warmed up we have any number of things we can do. We can do brushes, what the ballet dancer would call tendus, extending the leg from fifth position out into space, bringing it back very quickly. We also have something called plié-relevés, which begins with a plié. Then, while the knees are bent, you go up onto the balls of the feet, so that only the insteps work out. Then you straighten th knees, then you come down on the flat foot again. It's like a four-count exercise for the knees, for the feet and for the insteps as well. It gives you an introduction to balancing on the balls of the feet

Other things we do are our personal company warm-ups. We do a kind of plié, in which we extend the leg out and stand up on the standing foot, then bring the extended leg back to the neutral position. Which is actually an exercise for the hip setup and the lift in the torso so that you do not sag every time you plié. Going down into your lower space does not mean that you sag in the torso. It means that all the energy is suddenly concerned with its loweringness It's not a giving in, a retreat from upper space, which is what a sagging would be. It's not a surrender to gravity, it is a positive going down.

Other things we do: leg swings, loose knee leg swings, forward and back and forward and back to get the hip joint working. It's really more important to get the hip placed on top of the standing le as the working leg is working. We do balances on half toe as a way o working on our sense of upper space. A balance for us is not a perching on the ball of the foot but rather a lifting up into the space above you so strongly that you are actually lifted onto the ball of you foot. So that the heel practically floats off the floor and you're going up to the ball of your foot. I think good teachers of ballet teach the same thing, even if they don't use the concept of space. They say lift, float that heel off the floor so that you rise on to the ball of the foot.

And they always say lift from the hip.

Right. Very important. We stretch out the front of the hip, which is a very tight place on most people's bodies. We stretch that out so that we can lift along the front of it rather than being caved in toward the back.

Okay. Now my next question is, what does being a dance captain mean?

Well, different things to different companies. The dance captain is roughly synonymous with the ballet master. In our company the dance captain runs the rehearsals, is in charge of reviving old pieces if that's what the job at hand is, and is a liaison between the company and Murray if there is some discussion that has to go on. Also, I teach most of the master classes that Murray doesn't teach. In our company, it just means I'm the one who's been around the longest. It's not any great honor. I have more experience than anyone else because I'm the only one left over from the old company. We've been reviving *Bach Suite* and I'm the only one who's danced it before. So I'm the only one who knew the steps from before, and even though we revive it from the film, I can say, "We changed that from the last time we danced it." Then Murray can look at it and fiddle with it as he wants to restage it. The main thing is the rehearsals, if Murray's not there.

What does running the rehearsals entail?

there are any questions, I'm the one who is supposed to answer them, even if I don't have an answer. Or I'm the one who says, "All right now, we're going to run through *Personnae*," and everyone makes a wry face and says, "We don't really have to run through that," and I say, "Yes, we have to run through that because, because."

You mean you keep a list in your head of things that have to be done?

Yes. In our company it's very informal. I really go in as blank as anyone else, and they start asking me questions about what we're going to do today. Then I go to Murray and say, "Well, what are we going to do today?" And we do it.

But you're in everything, so you can't see it.

Right. I can only sit out if we're rehearsing an old repertory piece which I'm very secure in myself. If it's something fairly recent, I have to rehearse it myself and that's not good. In that sense any company needs a ballet master or mistress who sits out and watches and conducts the rehearsal with an outsider's eye. I wish we had somebody like that. It would be very valuable for us, because when we're in town Murray always has office business to take care of, and he can't always be in on the run-throughs and the rehearsals of pieces that really need looking at. We plead with him to come and look, and he says, "I can't, I have to do this and this and this." Sometimes we even get lazy and say, "Let's put this off until some other time." Then later he comes in to see how it looks and it doesn't look so hot. And then he gets concerned that it is not going to look good in performance.

How often do you have to rehearse a work?

That depends on the work. If it's new choreography we rehearse it as much as possible. For instance, after this three-week interim we're going to be taking out *Porcelain Dialogues, Personnae,* and *Hoopla* again. To do that, we have to run through *Porcelain* two or three times, *Personnae* once, and *Hoopla* not at all. It's a question of how much they have been performed and how much detail you have to pay attention to in each of the pieces.

And what about Scheherazade?

Well, we'll have to run through *Scheherazade* three times at least— once for recall, once for reconstruction, and once for polish. For myself, I try never to run through a thing just marking the steps. I tr to really perform each time. Sometimes you're working on a number of things and you can't lend that much energy to each run-through. But I learn more when I rehearse as though there's an audience out there and I'm getting across what I have to. After you've performed professionally for a while, to simply mark the steps for accuracy is not important any more. Particularly in our repertory, the important thing is not accuracy; it's communication. So you work on transitions, you work on the little things, and you can only do that at performing pitch. If you're not lending as much energy as a performance would call for, the energies are wrong and you have nothing to base your transition on if the thing before it hasn't been there, you see. So it's very valuable to rehearse at performing pitch.

On the other hand, it's hard to get yourself to a performing pitch without an audience. You get spoiled dancing for an audience. In the old days, dance companies rehearsed for eleven and a half months and performed for two weeks a year. Those dancers had to have such faith and such inner strength in order to rehearse that length of time, and their performance had to be startling in its impact. Otherwise they made no impact at all. We're spoiled because we can almost experiment with our pieces in front of an audience. You learn more from performing in front of an audience than from a year of classes.

I think this is why I'm disturbed when people won't go to see a dance because they've already seen it. Most things you haven't begun to see if you've seen them only once.

It depends upon the level at which a dance is choreographed and performed. Murray's stuff is nicely structured and it's good to look at. The first time you say, "That's a good piece." The second time you begin to see the subtleties. Then you see how the subtleties change from performance to performance—which, if you're a dedicated dance watcher, becomes a great fascination in itself.

I like watching the pieces again and again for almost the same reasons you like to perform them.

The performance really involves all your technique and all your training and the choreography and the audience. The audience is that final thing that makes a performance live. After all your preparation, all your energies being directed in the proper way, then crossing the gap and communicating with the audience, that's what walls off the experience of performing from all other kinds of experience.

A writer has to entrust his communicative efforts to paper; he doesn't have to be present for the moment of communication. We have to be. Any performing artist knows the feeling of the electric moment between performers and audience. People who are not performers don't realize that as an audience they have a responsibility to send the vibrations back to the performers, not only in the form of applause but in the form of attention. Dancers always prefer to perform for other performers because the other performers realize they are a sounding board that sends vibrations back to the performers. On the stage you are in a very vulnerable position. If you are sending out all this energy and all these vibrations and receiving nothing back, if people are just sitting back and yawning, it's deadly and depressing as hell. There can be any number of reasons for that, like the unsophistication of the audience.

The Sun Valley audience was a good example of that.

Right. That's a resort; the people are there to enjoy themselves; they don't want to come to a performance and have to contribute something. In an art performance, the audience might contribute a great deal of what's happening at the moment, even if they don't realize it. If you're to be thrilled by a piece of music you really can't sit back in a cushy chair. You do have to keep a fairly straight spine and an attentive ear. Your eye can't wander all over. The concentration is palpable. The audience sends it out and the performers sense it coming to them on stage.

The audience can read energy much more subtly than it imagines it can. All these books on body awareness are making people realize that just by looking at a person sitting in a chair you know certain attitudes they have about themselves, certain attitudes they have about others. Crossed legs and hands held in prayerful poses bespeak attitudes. An audience at a dance performance can be bamboozled by the event—the lights, the curtains, the people around them—and fail to read what they are seeing. They are instead tricked into thinking that they're seeing great art or drama unfolding. They read the program notes and think something happened because they read it in the program, not because they saw it with their own eyes. And it wasn't there, and so they were bamboozled.

Sometimes program notes give the audience too much to go on so that they're not going to think, or they're going to expect more than they will see.

The notes channel them. A lot of people want to be channeled. I suppose writers who write about the pieces would rather have

something they can start from. I think a choreographer should just
keep quiet.

Certain dance companies pretend to art when they merely serve
up entertainment. They do well-crafted dances of great entertainment
value and then in press releases or in program notes they pretend to
artistic universality which is simply not there. That makes me mad.
We never provide a program note because we want people to just
come and look. Which is what Edward Villella says in his radio ads
for the New York City Ballet: "Simply come and look." Well, there's
nothing wrong with that.

*I think that's the way to go to dance. I get asked a lot of questions by
people who don't know anything about dance, and they say, "I don't
know how to look."*

The unfamiliarity of the movement they're seeing also puts them off,
because they're not used to seeing a body move that way. I think
they're scared off. They could simply see something with a fresh eye,
but they're not used to seeing anything that way. It's either
predigested like television or monumentalized like a work of art.

What do you think can overcome that?

Exposure! See more. Whenever a dance company comes to town, go
and see it. Learn what's good, learn what's bad simply by watching.
Say to your neighbor, "I hated that," and then hope that your
neighbor will say, "Why?" Then you have to think, "Why did I hate
that?"

Dance is spreading out. Dance mania is happening all over the
country, which is good for audiences. It's tough on dance companies
because you get away less and less with your pretensions and you are
left more and more with what is actually there. So there will be less
phoniness, there will be more people who can spot phoniness. That's
the good thing. But phonies will always be there.

*Do you find big differences between a New York audience and an
audience out in Nebraska or Oklahoma?*

Of course. The audiences which are not used to coming to the
theater, the audiences in Oklahoma and Nebraska, are awed by the
occasion, by the people, by the formality. They are uncomfortable
because they don't know how to respond, they don't know what they

are supposed to do. And so they are timid about their response even if they like what they're seeing. It's very hard to get a laugh sometimes. Or it's hard to make them applaud even at the very end and even if they want to.

In more sophisticated outlying centers like university towns there's less awe. People are used to gathering in large numbers for an event, and they are more open to the thing that's happening in front of them and respond to that, rather than to the circumstances. New York has a big theater-going audience. Makarova was right when she said the other day that New Yorkers are a bit overindulgent. They will applaud wildly anything that's done professionally and with polish. A thing can be done badly, inartistically, but if it is pulled off with polish the New Yorkers will applaud it wildly, always. New Yorkers are great to perform for because they are so enthusiastic. But they don't distinguish between the genuine, artistic, poetic moment and the polished approximation of it.

In America our best audiences have always been college kids because they aren't corrupted by so much theater-going that they are blasé. If they don't like a thing, they won't respond. Usually they do respond to our stuff, which is a compliment, I think. We have been touring since 1969 and this crop of kids has gotten over its addiction to television and so their responses are not governed by a television response.

Now, a television response is a small response in the privacy of your own living room. You can sit there in pajamas with a beer in your hand and say in a flat voice, "Oh, I really liked that." A theater audience is in a much less comfortable situation and its response is expected to be vocal, quite loud, either positive or negative. That's part of the excitement of being in a crowd. You become part of a larger response and you can make yourself felt *en masse,* and that's very satisfying too. Whereas provincial audiences, used to being entertained only by television, make their responses minimal.

Does the theater itself make a difference?

Sometimes architecturally the theater is not conducive to a

The leg thrust carries the body forward into space. (*l. to r.:* Robert, Bill, Michael, Dan)

give-and-take. If there's a long distance between the audience and the performer, that's not good for the performer. I like to perform in small theaters because the response from the audience is so immediate and intimate.

Perhaps *the* most intimate theater I've ever performed in, the most intimate stage, is the Tyrone Guthrie Theater in Minneapolis. Strangely enough, it has a thrust stage, a three-quarter round stage, which our repertory is not choreographed for. We've adapted a number of our pieces for that stage. But it's built architecturally so that if you sit in any seat in the house your eye automatically drops to the stage. It feels wrong to sit in your seat and be looking around at the rest of the audience; you are focused right on the stage. Standing on that stage with a house full of people is an incredible experience because all that energy goes zoop, right on you. You know everything you do is seen. That's a marvelous feeling if you're secure in what you are doing. If you're insecure, I should think it would be ghastly. Sitting in that audience is also mârvelous because none of the seats are very far from the stage and you get a great feeling of rapport with the performers. I saw a play there once which was wonderful; you're almost sitting in the laps of the performers.

There are so many copies of that theater all over the country which have failed. We have played such dismal copies of that theater. I think the Guthrie is probably the prototype of those theaters that attempt to achieve intimacy with a three-quarter round stage, and they don't work. I don't know what the architect of the Guthrie did right, but something was right.

How did you like the Jacob's Pillow stage?

The theater has a nice intimate feeling. The stage is a bit small, but that barnlike building is so attractive to us city dwellers that you get a rustic, friendly, warm feeling right away. It's a good house. At NYU the audience was a little too close because the front row is right smack up against the stage, and you need a bit of distance in order to let your eye see what's going on around the stage. But I do like small houses. I much prefer them to the huge theaters.

Opera houses?

Some opera houses in Europe are designed with that intimate enclosed feeling. I remember particularly Wiesbaden in Germany and

Zagreb in Yugoslavia. They're large houses but they still have an intimate feeling, as opposed to Royce Hall on the UCLA campus, which is like performing into a tunnel.

Do you have a special size stage that you like? For example Robert [Small] said that the Jacob's Pillow stage was much too small for him because he's so tall.

I would prefer the playing area of the stage to be no smaller than thirty-five feet wide and thirty feet deep. If it's any smaller than that it starts to be cramped. We like to have a lot of depth because the cyclorama at the back needs to be dark in order to receive the slides, and if it's pushed too far forward the other stage lights shine onto it and wash out the slides. A lot of depth gives a greater sense of freedom and lets you run very deeply into the stage and come back. I should say a thirty-five by thirty-foot playing area is a good minimum and that doesn't include the apron in front or wing space on the sides. Larger than that is nice too. I don't think the NYU stage was thirty-five feet wide, maybe it was. Terrible depth problems there.

Sometimes as a member of the audience you can enjoy a performance very much that the performer doesn't think was such a good one. And sometimes the performer can really like a performance that you as a member of the audience don't get as much out of. Why is that?

Some performances the dancers enjoy incredibly more than others—performances of the same piece. The people in the audience are quite often of a different opinion. There are certain satisfactions which the dancers have as performers. One of them is performing a thing with accuracy, with a phrasing, a sense of flow through the piece which delivers a kind of continuity to the performer. Phrasing and continuity are difficult things to work with because they're so insubstantial. You can't just decide that you're going, for example, to work on continuity tonight. It almost happens as a result of everyone's chemistry or everyone's frame of mind being just right and as a result of going through a piece in a certain very organic way without having to force anything.

    Now if you're sitting in the audience and watching that very same piece, the organic development is not what you notice. Because of its developing according to its own rules, things are going correctly and you have a sense of well-being from that. But you don't necessarily get excited about it, because it's not obvious to the eye, it's not a punchy kind of thing. What the audience sees are high points and great moments and these things stick in the mind as signposts indicative of the quality of the entire performance, whereas the dancers don't remember the high points. They remember the flow, the continuity.

The high points and the low points are momentary things which happen and then are gone. What the performer has to hang onto is his professional responsibility to the piece; it is important for him that it have this flow. In the audience you enjoyed a thing tremendously because there were moments of great personality, great charm. In *Proximities* particularly, the dancers have great opportunities to project their personal charm. Something strikes you as being wonderfully joyful and you relish that. It's a fact of life that personalities capture the audience much more readily than any strict artistic standards or other disciplines within the art. The performers have to be aware of all the disciplines at once, whereas the personality thing is a star quality, an extra bonus beyond the demands of the performance.

I think you all have very little of that.

Of what?

Personality. In the star sense, the ego sense.

Other people have accused us of being so much personality that it obscures the dancing.

They have? Who?

I don't remember. Maybe die-hard classicists from the Nikolais technique.

I don't think you do at all. I think there's so little obtrusive personality in Murray's company that unless you know the names you can't tell who's who. A general audience doesn't know who's who with the exception of where it is spelled out in the program. I've often wondered if that bothers you?

Bothers us? No. Marcia [Wardell] gets very disturbed about being a beautiful object on stage, because she wants to *be* the material rather than be someone executing the material. I know one dancer from our technique whose body is a marvelous, flexible instrument. He can *be* the space-time-motion thing rather than someone executing it. It is incredible to watch. But on the other hand it has no color. He does not impose any of his own experiential things on it. It simply is what it is.

To us, this ability to do the pure thing is astounding. Marcia wants to achieve that kind of clarity. My personal opinion is that to be pure is like distilled water. It has no taste. In a classroom that's what you're working for. But in a classroom you're probably also trying to work the mud out of your system so that you can attain a kind of clarity, a kind of purity. There is so much obstruction, so much ego or physical things that get in the way as you work for a purity. But I think to attain a purity is a little dull. However, I never thought about that before. That's interesting.

In the Nikolais company the direction is all in such abstract terms. Nikolais will choreograph the pieces on the dancers and ask them to execute it in such and such a way, using just the vocabulary —the space, time, shape, motion terms—and sometimes images; for example, of ants scurrying about or something like that. But that's a dynamic image, not a human or personality kind of image. It's certainly not an emotional or dramatic image. I don't think I ever remember Nikolais—well, maybe once—giving a dramatic image when he wanted to pull a thing out of you in performance. It's always interesting to watch the Nikolais company perform because some of them have that incredible clarity and they can deliver whatever Nikolais asks for, and sometimes if a dancer within the company is obsessed with his own ego, that's what comes out.

I think when we are talking about personality maybe we are talking about two different things. You said sometimes you are criticized for displaying personality on stage, whereas I think it's your personal qualities that come across.

Well, a dancer on the stage can't hide his personality even if he tries. Every time he moves he reveals himself. A lot of dancers are aware of this power, but they don't want to reveal themselves, they want to reveal an audience-pleasing personality. So they will plaster on a smile. Or, if you're doing a heavily dramatic dance, putting on long faces or looking down your nose or turning your eyes up to heaven is another example.

In our case you can't hide behind Murray's choreography because it has such clarity. With other choreographers if they've done a heavy dramatic dance you may be able to throw yourself into a state of emotion or a state of narrative wherein you don't have to reveal your own personality—you overlay a state of being, an emotion, an acting role on top of the movement. In Murray's choreography you don't get that kind of bush to hide behind, so you are left with the choreography. And a lot of this comes in: how you handle movement to turn it into motion; how you attack it; what kind of energy you attack it with or whether you put a heavy emphasis into it; how you handle your transitions particularly, because Murray leaves the transitions up to the dancers. You reveal yourself openly in your handling of transitions.

Murray wants us to handle all these things in a craftsmanlike manner, not indulging ourselves and not skipping over things without giving them enough thought. If you are fully engaged in the motion, you go into those transitions out of what has come before and you find the most kinetic way to go into the next thing. By "kinetic" I mean you are aware of the laws of physics and gravity and momentum that are involved and you use them in a witty, pungent way, in order to bring out the thing you're about to do after the transition. It takes a lot of experience to do that.

So that any plastered-on personality ruins it?

Precisely. No matter what you do to hide or obfuscate it, the personality comes out. Now, in our choreography there are parts where you have the opportunity simply to grin at the audience and try to be lovable. Those are the danger spots for us, and I think sometimes we give in to them.

Do you give in to them because the audience makes you?

Because you know the audience likes it. Murray himself is an audience-oriented choreographer. He wants the dance company to be ravishing enough so that the audience wants to go along with it. And so he has a beautiful company. But there's a danger that the beauty and the audience seduction will become more important than the

In rehearsal for *Geometrics* going from a static moment to a lift. (*l. to r.:* Michael-Janis, Robert-Dianne, Dan-Anne, Bill-Sara)

work. It makes him furious when the kinetics get lost and the concern with the material gets lost. A certain amount of playing to the audience is fine. It makes the audience more comfortable, more receptive. There's nothing more off-turning to an audience than glacial dancers or an attitude of superiority or hauteur unless, perhaps, the material is spectacular, like ballet. Then you don't need personality, all you need are those whizzing turns and those leaps in the air, which are satisfying, in a way.

Our choreography has spectacular elements, but that's not the point of it, so we have to watch out for those passages, particularly in the pieces with classical music. Classical music will lull the audience into a sense of security about the event. They are not being assaulted by unfamiliar sounds. In Nikolais's pieces he always uses his own electronic sound because he doesn't want the audience to be lulled by the sound. He always wants them on the edge of their seats or at least sitting up straight, not falling asleep to Tchaikovsky. Murray takes the chance with the classical music because he is a romantic. But then the performers can't sit on the music and indulge themselves.

When you are playing this personality game it's self-indulgence, it feeds your narcissism because it makes the audience love you. Agnes de Mille talks about that very well. She was talking about using performance as almost a sexual encounter because of that mass love. Probably great stars in any performing field get that mass love coming toward them, and it's very satisfying at the moment. But I suspect it palls and you keep having to have new doses of that mass love in order to feel that you are worthwhile. That may be the danger of being a great star. You have to keep it coming toward you. Being a star is having the peculiar quality that goes out to the audience in order to generate that love or that attention. All stage work has that danger in it.

I don't find that personality is the issue at all in the dances. I don't think you are obtrusive personalities in real life either. It seems to me that the Murray Louis Dance Company has that pretty well under control.

That's true, there are not a lot of peculiarities. The first company I was in of Nikolais's had personalities. There was Bill Frank and Murray and Phyllis Lamhut and Luly Santangelo and Batya Zamir.

These people were strong personalities. It was interesting to have them all working together too. I was terrified because I didn't have the personality to stand up to their kind of assault, so I formulated the rule for myself to keep my mouth shut when working and always be in the right place at the right time so that no one could yell at me and say, "What are you doing there?" I really got quite timorous after the first couple of weeks of rehearsal because I kept getting yelled at.

How long did it take before you could become assertive?

Assertive? Even now I'm not very assertive, and I'm supposed to be dance captain.

But it's a thin line between being a personality and—

Being strong enough for a stage presence? Maybe not so thin. Taking into account the variety of personalities that make up a company, there's really quite a broad spectrum of aggressiveness or shyness and various qualities of compensating. If you feel you're excessively shy you might act excessively brash. Or if you think people are not liking you because you are too outgoing you might pull back a little and affect a shyness that you don't have.

In performance?

In performance, absolutely, because you feel those things about yourself. I've always been very shy, so I might assert myself more on the stage because I never had the chance in life. Also, as you accumulate experience you know when to assert yourself and when not to assert yourself. But it is dangerous, particularly in Murray's choreography, where the work is the most important thing. If he had wanted a company of personalities, he would have worked differently. About a year ago we were really into personalities, but then we got a shakedown and he started yelling at us. So we stopped that. It's a human frailty. You want to be onstage and you want to show off.

What about dancing in Scheherazade?

I love doing that role. It was really choreographed for me, on me. And I think Murray was taking out a lot of his romantic yearnings through me because he saw the same thing in me that he has in himself, a kind of nineteenth-century romantic response to music and to situations. So it suits me; therefore, I go into it with great confidence. I've always hated the backstage business where people come back and say, "It was so wonderful." But people would start to come backstage and say, "That was really remarkable." And for a long time I held myself off and didn't let it affect me much.

Then people I really respected started coming backstage and saying that. Nikolais would come—and when Nikolais gives you a compliment like that it makes your heart tremble—and Hanya Holm comes back and gives compliments and Phyllis Lamhut. Those big three, who you know aren't going to say what they don't mean. And that affected me in another way. It made me hungry for more big roles because I feel that I can tackle them now. I'd like to do big roles. I still don't feel that I'd like to choreograph; I'm only an apprentice at that. Anyway, doing big roles feeds your ego. I'm trying to keep a leash on my ego as far as *Scheherazade* is concerned. But everybody keeps complimenting me. I'm now trying to avoid having people gush over me. Initially, it made me uncomfortable because I don't want to let it carry me away. To my friends I just say, "Hush, I don't want to talk about it."

What kind of big roles do you want to do?

Just solo roles. I didn't find out until I actually had solo roles that it's a whole other challenge to be a soloist. In the corps, your challenge is to mold your personal expressiveness to the demands of the group so that you don't stand out in a sore thumb kind of way. You can shine within what you're doing but you have quite limited boundaries within which you can shine. That's a great challenge for a performer. But when you get into the soloist role you find you have loads of freedom to work with the material in either way you want to, whether in the motional way or the personality way. There's the fascination in being able to take your own measure, try your wings, find out how far you can trust yourself to go. How much you can draw on your own dancing experience, your knowledge of the body, and how far it can go within the laws of physics. How many turns you can take or how daring a balance you can achieve, how much time—timing is very important in solo roles because the timing is left almost completely up to you.

That's what I do in *Scheherazade.* I'm dancing to the Rimsky-Korsakov and I'm the only thing on stage. I don't have to bow to the music and I don't have to bow to the group. It fascinates

me to be able to play within the time and with the energy. In
Scheherazade I come on at the end of the first act after a whole lot
of stuff has gone on, and I feel compelled because of what has gone
on before to really sock out what I have to do. It's a brief little bit
before the curtain comes down on the first act, and I feel compelled
to hit it hard. I know I shouldn't because, the way it's set up, I don't
have to knock it out. But I do. After two minutes I come off stage
panting and sweating and I know that I should not be doing that
because I don't have to. I sit offstage watching what's going on and
hearing the sounds, and this thing starts to build up, this sense that I
have to go on and have to top it. Yet I really don't have to. I can top
it without knocking myself out. But I still knock myself out and I can
criticize myself on that kind of performance. I think maybe once in
the New York run I felt that I had done it correctly within the
demands of the piece.

So as a soloist you can work with all that kind of stuff and then
go into the drama too. Scheherazade has a very definite personality,
an exotic kind of hauteur. Scheherazade controls the stage. Whenever
I'm on, Scheherazade controls what's going on. I have to find out
how much of what I do is Murray's conception, and how much there
is of my conception. I'm beginning to find out. It's a wish fulfillment.
Anybody who is shy always wants to control the situation and I
suppose I get a great deal of satisfaction out of being able to gesture
with my arm and have six people fall over just because of that gesture.
It's a marvelous feeling. Maybe it's a personal catharsis, doing that
role, because it's the fulfillment of a dream.

As for other solo pieces that I would like to do, Murray
choreographed his Ravel piece, *Moment,* on me. I was the understudy
for him and for Nureyev. I felt that I accomplished that role in the
short time I had to do it, and I would love to do that role in front of
an audience. Technically and physically it's not exhausting at all, and
yet it's quite exhausting because there is so much detail and so much
quality work, and there is a dramatic thread that you have to keep in
mind all the time. That took a lot of mental effort as well as the
physical work, and it was very satisfying. And then Murray said I
danced it well, and that was nice too.

But you'll be doing Moment, *won't you?*

I'll be doing the corps part, not the solo part.

Ever?

Ever. It's not my role, it's Murray's role. He choreographed it for Nureyev but with the idea that he was going to perform it. You see, he hasn't had a big solo role since *Chimera* in 1966. He needed a new solo role. He's been thinking of one for at least three years now, and finally it comes out. Solo with group. But that's all right.

*If you
want to
communicate,
you have to
find out
what
communicates*

Abstract and Dramatic Gesture
Conviction
Stage Experience
The German Technique
Dancing the Dances
Watching Dance

This conversation took place in New York City
during the Christmas holidays. To escape from the
hurly-burly of the season we borrowed the office of a
psychiatrist friend on Riverside Drive, in order to find
a quiet place to talk.

What are the differences among abstract gestures, dramatic gestures,
and symbolic gestures?

Let's take the gesture of an arm being lifted up and extended out to
another person. As an abstract gesture the arm is lifted, it weighs a
certain amount, it goes through a certain amount of space, it takes a
certain amount of time. With a certain amount of energy it stretches
out in the direction of another person. And that's all you can say
about it, abstractly. All these things are accomplished in order that
the arm finally stretches out toward another person through the space.

Symbolically, stretching out the hand and the arm to another
person stands for an offer of help. As a symbol that's what the gesture
is. A lot of people accept a symbolic gesture as being a theatrically
dramatic event when actually it's a conventionally agreed upon
symbol.

Dramatically, you have to fit the gesture into the context of what
is going on. The other person is in difficulty, he is down on the floor
and he can't get up. The hand stretched out is an offer of help from
another human being. It may be an offer not only of help but an offer
of some other kind of involvement, a love involvement or even a

financial involvement. All these things are embellishments to the basic abstract gesture.

Or take the concept of frustration. A gesture that symbolizes frustration in our culture may not symbolize frustration in the Japanese Noh drama. However, there are certain abstract gestures which are in themselves, frustrated—one set of muscles working against another set of muscles so that no movement is possible. The arm wishes to reach out but another set of muscles wishes to pull the arm back, and so there's an inherent frustration of the gesture. Within the framework of abstract principles you can understand what frustration means; not being able to accomplish what the intent is.

Dramatically, frustration fits into a whole context. Maybe another person will frustrate the gesture of help by breaking in and interrupting the arm stretching out. All these things have to be considered. The idea is that there are certain kinds of frustration. The audience has to feel that it happens symbolically, or kinetically, or as a state of mind in the performers. There are all these considerations, and that's what makes a theatrical performance so rich—all these layers and different resonances.

It's difficult to look at abstraction as such.

It's difficult to cut through the eye's habit of attaching meaning to everything it sees, particularly in terms of human movement. In our lives we are always watching people moving, and interpreting to ourselves what they are doing. If people are on stage doing an abstract dance, you see gestures which in your past you have interpreted as being symbols of certain feeling states or certain dramatic situations, like the hand going out to another person. It can be very difficult to cut away all your associations and simply see that as a kinetic line.

Murray is very specific about what kind of gesture we are to use. He gets angry with us when we try to interpret the drama of what's going on. He has torn into us on a couple of occasions for trying to substitute an emotive kind of presentation as opposed to fully exploring the movement material he's given us, in all the senses of our technique—the space, the time, the motional values of the movement —thereby illuminating the idea. That puts an awful load on his head because he has to make sure that the movement is right for the statement. We, as performers intuit what is needed from the material. As a matter of fact, when he was choreographing *Catalogue* he used almost exclusively dramatic images for the girl's solos. One was "frustrated," one was "driven," and he actually titled those solos with those words. Then the girls began to put that dramatic emphasis into it, and he saw a performance of it and decided that that was not the way they should go about performing their solos.

Murray has been trained in the abstract tradition—he doesn't trust dramatic dancing. At least one member of his company and maybe some of the others are very fine dramatic dancers, although trained almost exclusively in the abstract tradition. Annie [McLeod] is a fine dramatic dancer and would actually prefer to approach a role that way. But Murray won't let her, and I think he's right, considering what he wants to do with his work. Also, in the first act of *Scheherazade* there are dramatic things going on. So Murray has to resolve when he should let a thing be interpreted dramatically and when he should insist on the abstract dealing with motion.

How do you put feelings into something that is neutral or abstract?

The movement is given to you. You can color that any way you want.

But it puts the solid burden on you.

Yes. It's very satisfying to the performers, if they are given a thing like that, to have the choreographer tell them to take the movement and shade it, color it with wistfulness and anxiety, or something like that. In our technique this happens. The performer is free to lend to the thing whatever richness he has within himself—coming out of his own life experience. In our company we trust Murray Louis as a choreographer strongly enough so that we know we have a structure there, and if we stick to the structure of the movement, a certain thing will have happened and we are in control of how the audience can respond, whether on a positive-negative, happy or sad, or tense shading of the structure.

In other words you choose the how.

You choose the how. Murray will look at it and say, "I agree with this part and this part, but that is a little too obvious and in the other part you've gone off on your own trip when it doesn't necessarily have anything to do with what I'm saying. So pull it in a little here and let it out a little there."

During the past week I've been going to the studio to watch Nikolais teach the Christmas course. It's fascinating. Yesterday he kept telling the students to take the ideas out of their compositions. How do you get to be that pure?

It's very difficult, and the nice thing about Nikolais's teaching is that he demands it from the very first, so that you really never get a chance to do those grandiose dances that you go into dance wanting to do. Maybe that's just as well. He's concerned that his students learn the basic craft first, that they learn the materials, what they have to work with, the uses of dynamics. It's invaluable. There's no going wrong if you have a grasp of all those things. Then you can say, I want to express sadness through the use of the body. What kind of time sense is sad? It's slow. Maybe slow with quick rushes of dynamic punctuations. The same with shapes. What kind of weight in the body is sad? Then you can go ahead and use all that you've acquired in order to express sadness. The choreographer has to be prepared when he feels he has a statement to make. He has to have the materials, just as a painter has to have paint and easel and canvas and brushes and things like that in order to make his painting.

I was interested in how hard it was for the students to get it down to the purest possible thing.

That's because they had probably already had two or three years of dance training and they came with preconceptions. But if you start children right into abstraction they pick it up with no problem. A lot of dance students have to unlearn all the more advanced concepts which they think should go into dance. They want to make their statements first, they want to do a feminist dance first. They can do that after, I think. If they're interested in dance they should probably learn the materials of dance. If they're interested in women's lib maybe they should go out and work with the women's movement or something like that. Then do the feminist dance. But I suppose it's a human condition to be involved in several scenes at once; you want to be a dancer and be a libber at the same time. If you're working in art forms I should think you would want to get to the basics first.

I don't think a lot of people think that way.

It's the hard way. It's much easier to get out on the stage and be passionate about what you want to do. But it doesn't work nearly so well for an audience. I suppose something else is also involved— whether you are concerned in communicating to an audience or whether you are concerned in just expressing your own feeling, just getting it out of yourself. That's another function of drama and dance, but I would call that therapy rather than art.

If you want to communicate you have to find out what communicates, and I think someone on stage does not communicate militancy just by feeling militant. Every speech-maker knows that. If they want to get an audience or crowd roused about something they have to use all kinds of little tricks. They have to build their sentences in certain ways. They have to use certain key phrases and words that will inflame the audience's imagination or arouse it to anger, or whatever they are trying to do. Like Nixon when he was campaigning on "law and order." Everyone was so sick of disorder by the end of the sixties that that was a fine catch phrase. It made everyone think that everything was going to be all right, yet it was meaningless until you got down to what was involved in establishing law and order. No one was prepared to go into that massive effort. ˙

When you travel all over the country and give classes, do you find that most people think of dance in terms of dramatic ideas rather than abstraction?

Not so much now. I'd say as recently as the late sixties people were still caught up in the idea of expressing themselves—doing emotional or dramatic or narrative dances and truly thinking that this was the only kind of dancing outside of, say, a style like ballet. They would be shocked when you did not even show interest in that kind of effort. In our concerts, because Murray is so audience-oriented and knows how to move an audience, he usually could win people to his side simply by the presentation of our concert material. But that didn't give choreographers and dance teachers any idea of how to go about doing it themselves.

Over the past five to ten years the whole emphasis has changed. The younger choreographers have gone out to the colleges and they've been teaching. The old guard of dramatic dancers head the dance departments but the younger people are the ones who are teaching the classes. There's a greater interest in the abstract concerns—the use of weight and time, physical forces, gravity, centrifugal force, things like that. Exploring these aspects with the body is fascinating to a number of people, and even if they don't put it into terms as explicit as that, that's what they're doing. Even the idea of pedestrian movement (which is everyday movement, organized) becomes an artistic expression of one kind or another. All these opinions are going back and forth, and we find there's little resistance to our kind of teaching methods or improvisation methods now because people realize that there are many ways of attacking a dance training problem.

And this is all in the last five years?

I would say in the last five years the shift has happened toward abstraction—toward at least a willingness to look into basic materials, rather than using a wallpaper of idea over the masonry of the craft.

People don't want to tell stories as much as they used to.

That's right. I think young people may be more realistic about themselves today than when I was a kid. They realize that they themselves don't have the experience, they aren't prepared to put a saga on the stage, or a symbolic journey into the soul. They're not ready for it because they are not yet acquainted with journeys into the soul.

One of the dance critics was saying that what is lacking now is the passion found in older dancers. They were fed by a conviction, a kind of intuitive approach to the problems of life and the soul, of living, of relationships—strongly sexual, sometimes mythic, sometimes playful interaction of personalities. There were such strong personalities in dance. The characters they were dancing were strong and the people who were doing it were strong.

Which often is missing from dance in general now.

Yes, it's rare now anywhere. I'm not old enough to know about the good old days, but I don't think there are as many great personalities around now as there were then. Perhaps because the old people had to fight so hard just to get on the stage they had to be strong, they had to have a belief that what they were doing was right. That was the only thing that got them on the stage. Now it's easier. There are dance companies that are established, there's a growing dance audience, and a higher technical level. You don't have to have that passionate conviction to get on the stage.

Do you think the dancers in Murray's first works were more dedicated than you all are now?

Yes I think they were. They had to be. We don't have to be because we can earn a living at dancing. They couldn't possibly earn a living doing it, and the only reason for them to dance was because they were convinced that it was the thing to be doing. We can get away with having our reservations and still enjoy dancing because we don't have to do anything else, we don't have to spend our energies making a living outside of what we are doing. I think that's it, in a nutshell. Any time you pay people to do something, they don't have to be totally convinced to be doing it. But something has been lost, I think.

Partly I think it's the times. The Second World War wiped out certain values of solidity and permanence. Then the fifties were more materialistic—big social changes. The sixties were uproarious, upturning all social values and moral values, and I think that has had an effect on the arts. Perhaps in the art world there's an emphasis on surface. You can get on the stage today by sheer, silky, glistening technique.

Those who have the conviction are still just as strong. Murray is one. He believes that the art must not be diluted, that sheer technique must not take the place of a true aesthetic expression, because then it becomes like a circus.

For instance, when we were at the Uris Theater I was standing offstage watching *Corsaire* with Fonteyn and Nureyev, just listening to the music. It is pure circus music.It's easy to be diverted into that because it's spectacular and it's interesting to watch, but it's superficial, on the level of spectacle. Now, I'm not saying that great artists could not make the *Corsaire* pas de deux an aesthetic moment (which they do). But from offstage, just sitting there letting my mind wander, I found that it was like being in a circus. The crowds unfortunately want more spectacle, and any performer will tend to give the audience what it's asking for.

I did want to ask you about dancing at the Uris and what that was like. [In November 1975 Hurok Concerts presented Dame Margot

Fonteyn, Rudolf Nureyev, Leslie Edwards, Daniel Lommel, and also Michael Ballard, Richard Haisma, Jerry Pearson, and Robert Small of the Murray Louis Dance Company, who performed with Nureyev in Louis's Moments.]

It was a whole experience which we're not brought up to expect because we're not into the superstar international scene. I went to rehearsals with Nureyev saying, "This won't affect me. I will do my job, I will be a professional. I will try to sustain on the stage what we have always been expected to sustain," which is that aesthetic continuum through the piece. But you find that someone as strong as Nureyev isn't just another person. People like that do have that something extra—that's what makes them stars. They have that passion, they have the personality, they have the crowds following them around and applauding them.

It was fascinating to watch Rudolf take bows. I found it most inspiring and really most touching because he gives every bit of himself during those bows. I could see the line of his back, how the energy was coming from way down deep *out* through his chest and through his arms and through his face. It was beautiful to see, and it taught me a lesson about going out to the audience. If you are a performer there's no holding back, for whatever reason—whether you're not feeling well that night, or the lights are not proper on stage, or something's a distraction.

It's so easy to be distracted and it's so rare when all the circumstances come together and you feel that you have sustained all the nuances and all the line, whether narrative or abstract, the whole length of the piece. If you've sustained everything all the way through without getting distracted, that's a life moment for the performer. Usually there's some kind of distraction, something that pulls you out. But when it all comes together, and the audience knows it and applauds, and you know it's the right applause, that's very moving for a performer.

It's a matter of concentration. If you can keep it going in yourself you're pretty sure that it will happen for the audience as well, given the performer's professional experience in getting things across. In Murray's company the stage experience varies fantastically from night to night. You're always alert and it's always interesting. You watch what's going on. In *Moments,* particularly, we just stand and look at Murray. There's one point where Richard [Haisma] and I are standing way upstage and Murray's downstage doing something. Richard is always very volatile about his appreciations of what's going on. If Murray does something particularly nice I'll hear "Ohh, oohh (snort, snuffle) wonderful," and I have to fight to keep a straight face because Richard is gasping in my ear.

What happened at the Uris?

We delivered at a level. Murray said we were perfectly fine, we were steadfast, we kept our level. That's really all he could have asked of us then, because Rudolf did not play to us. Which is all right. That's one way of looking at that piece, that he is not really too concerned with the figures [the four boys in the chorus.] That's the way Rudolf played it each time, and there was little variation from night to night. Murray plays with us much more, which is more interesting to us. So at the Uris we did our job, and it was nice to play on a big stage in front of a Broadway house, but I wouldn't want to continue doing it.

Do you think that ballet dancers are less apt to play and change within a piece?

Yes. I think in a tradition like ballet it's built into the performers that they do what is expected of them. Stars are expected to deliver more, so they do those few extra turns, they hold their balance that much longer. But it's probably because the ballet master or the choreographer has said to go out and knock it out, to do what they can. Otherwise they do what is expected of them. I think most classical training does not prepare a dancer to participate creatively in a performance, and we always do.

Have you read Beyond Technique *by Eric Bruhn?* [Dance Perspectives *36, Winter 1968]. Because Bruhn talks about that. People who have danced with him said they never knew what to expect from him. They always had to keep their eye on him because he would come out and do something totally unexpected and that would make them react. I once heard Cynthia Gregory say this about being in* Miss Julie *with Bruhn—that she learned so much from him because he was always making her aware by doing this.*

think that's very valuable, particularly if you have a drama in which characters interact. If you can keep each other on an edge of

spontaneity, that's always exciting for an audience and for a performer too.

I think Murray's things have that.

Sometimes to our dismay. In *Scheherazade* I've come off swearing at Murray, but we work it out. In the last duet he'll pull something. I'll get to the point where I'll say, "All right, you just do what you do and I'll go along with it," and he'll say "No, no, no, let's rehearse." So we rehearse, but I keep an eye on him. I'm still watching every moment; I don't let him throw me, because he has done it a couple of times.

How? By doing something totally unexpected?

Or leaving out a section of something. The final duet in *Scheherazade* is done to a tape loop which repeats itself and repeats itself. It's quite long, and if toward the beginning he's left out a whole section of what he's supposed to do, when we come toward the end where we think the music is going to change and it doesn't, we're stuck there and left on our own. That's where our improvisational skill comes in.

How do you tell on a tape loop where the end is? How do you time the whole thing?

In the case of the *Scheherazade* duet there's no telling. The movement takes a certain time and toward the end of the movement you think it's time for the music to change, and usually it does. The timing of the movement is almost always exact, so it's a big surprise when it's not exact.

When you say timing of the movement what do you mean?

Duration. How long the movement takes.

But can't that change?

It changes, but it's quite consistent. Really. The structure of at least the first part of the final duet in *Scheherazade* is that I do a thing

Here the shape of the body is secondary to the space outside the body *(Schubert)*. *(l. to r.:* Bill, Dan, Robert)

Energy is shot out to the audience as personality *(Glances)*. *(l. to r.:* Sara, Michael, Helen)

and he does a thing and I do a thing and he does a thing. There is a beat in the music but it's not counted. We just do it, and we feel free to take up as much time as we want to. Sometimes Murray has been known to get carried away, and then we're a little short at the end. But it helps when you're creating the movements. When Murray creates movement you can have a little lag section at the end where you're left to improvise on certain themes until you hear the music cue which takes you into the next section. There is a section in that duet when Murray goes stage left and I go stage right and we work on various themes until we hear the next music cue, which in that case is where the Rimsky-Korsakov comes in. Then we start doing things together again. Sometimes that free time is longer and sometimes it's shorter.

How did he choreograph that section? Which came first, the music or the movement?

The movement came first. I'm trying to remember if he ever had any other musical ideas for that section. I don't think so. It was choreographed quite some time ago. But after he had put a tape loop to it, we do have certain things that are counted because there is a strong beat in it, and we decided it was best to keep us together because we can't always see each other. We're kept together by staying with that beat, and then we break up. We don't pay any attention to it any more, but the span of each section of movement seems to take the same amount of time.

Is that the same as the Gold Trio? [The company name for the Balancing Act in Hoopla].

Yes. In Copenhagen [setting *Hoopla* on the Royal Danish Ballet] the trio ran out of music halfway through so Murray had to add almost the whole thing over again on tape.

I wanted to ask you about teaching in Copenhagen.

The dancers are wonderful in their ability to pick up movement. They are also wonderful in their ability to make it look good on stage, professionally well done.

When you say pick up movement, do you mean learn the steps?

Yes, and they're very good at doing that. *Proximities* was never performed spatially. Well, I saw only their first two performances. We almost didn't bother to teach them a spatial concept because we knew it would take much more time than we had to give them that concept. When they had a swinging of the arm out into space, I tried to tell them about having a piece of chalk on the end of their finger and drawing a line with the end of their finger which they watched with their eye all the time. That's a fairly simple concept to pick up —a circumference kind of peripheral action in space.

They picked that up fine, but the idea of energy shooting out into and creating a larger space around the performer takes a long time to pick up. It takes a long time even to conceive, and we just didn't have enough time. So what we got was a professional-looking, pleasant rendition of the steps, which was all right, but it left me disenchanted—and I think it also left Murray disenchanted—with the idea of spreading his repertory over other companies, because it can't be done. Now he's interested in choreographing specifically for other companies, in which case he can take into account all the limitations. For instance, he can use the massive forces of a big ballet company and put on spectacles, which is interesting for someone who has never had more than nine people in his company.

Murray, if he knows the limitations, can always work within them. If he thinks he's free to do a spatial dance he'll do that. He's always threatening to make his choreography dancer-proof. In other words, if the dancers just do the steps it'll look good and it'll come out what he intends. It will be interesting if he actually comes up with something like that. It sounds a little suspicious to me, because, of late, I would say from *Index* on, his choreography has been almost totally dependent on the strong performing ability of his dancers. Earlier pieces like *Calligraph for Martyrs* will transfer to a ballet company very well because it's just step, step, step, step. The impact of it and the structure of it are so solid that dancers almost can't ruin it, if they do the steps. *Bach Suite* is loaded with steps, I mean there's nothing but steps in it. You can make it much richer by the use of spatial considerations, and he insists on that from us, of course. He wants all the ramifications of space and shape and motional thrust.

wanted to talk about Bach Suite *because Murray was telling me*

*about rehearsing it in Florida. He said everybody had to get beyond a
certain point with it, and he felt no one had gotten beyond that point.*

That was so painful.

So he said. Tell me about it.

We were having an open rehearsal in front of an audience so that we
would have a feeling for an audience, and it was interesting for the
dance students there. Also Murray wanted to see us do it in front of
an audience. Well, *Bach Suite* is based on the old technique, as we
call it—the technique that was inherited from Hanya Holm through
Nikolais—of spatial patterns rather than a more intuitive use of space.
We use space very subtly, whereas that piece was based on actual
patterns of space which you described with parts of your body and
which you indicated with your eye focus and your chest focus. It's a
very strong form dance, and all these forms can be lightly or very
strongly touched, depending on the performers. Murray wanted it all
very explicit, as they had done it in the old days—consciously drawing
all the lines on the space, consciously directing the spatial attention
this way and that way.

From the film we learned the steps, and we spent a lot of time
arguing about steps and learning it and learning it. When Murray
finally came in to watch it, he was appalled. He saw none of that
strong, old-style technique of spatial use because it's not apparent
from the film image. He had forgotten that we were now used to
working with a more delicate nuance. So he laid into us. We just
listened open-mouthed. Then he had to go through it with us beat by
beat to find out all the spatial implications. It was terribly difficult and
terribly discouraging because every second of the time you have to be
aware of what's going on spatially.

Finally, when it came time for doing it in Florida we'd been
doing master classes and lecture demonstrations every day, as well as
rehearsing in the afternoons, so we were all very tired. We did
everything twice. We went on and did *Bach Suite,* and then Robert
Small and Helen Kent did *Facets,* then we did *Bach Suite* again, then
somebody else did *Facets.* Poor Helen. After she had done *Bach Suite*
the second time, she was down on the floor and her body went into
shock because she had pushed harder and gone further than she'd
ever done before in dancing. She was in a cold sweat and shaking and

crying, so we fed her candy to get sugar into her system and covered
her up and kept her warm and all that, and she bounced back quickly.
But she had been through a physical trauma. You push your mental
faculties and your physical faculties further than they've ever gone
before in order to accomplish that thing which you haven't
experienced before and which that old-style technique demands
because it's so exact and so strong that it can't be done any other
way. Otherwise it's just watered down again.

That was very painful, particularly for Helen because she wasn't
expecting that kind of shock. But she said later that it was a
marvelous experience. As for me, I was dragged out, so tired I could
hardly move. I think everyone else felt the same way. It was painful
to be pushed through that, but we had to. Then the first performance
here in New York seemed so light and so easy by comparison that we
were astounded, and yet people who sat in the audience were
delighted because they saw what was happening; the intent of the
piece was made evident. In the two performances since then it's
gotten stronger each time. And it makes you wonder whether it
always has to be so hideously hard at first in order that it be easy or
second nature afterward. I guess it does.

Yet in a piece like *Scheherazade* I wonder if Murray tapped into
something that was there in me and just brought it out. It was always
fairly easy for me and in terms of numbers of turns and balances and
things like that I just go along and increase and hone down. But it
was never a trauma for me, perhaps because it was choreographed on
me. I think that Murray now likes to choreograph specifically for the
people who are going to do the dance.

*But didn't he do that in the old days too? Part of the reason I wanted
to ask about* Bach Suite *is something Phyllis Lamhut was saying
yesterday. She felt that when the old company did it, it was stronger
than yours and much more lyrical. She said that yours was very light.*

That's true, we are lighter. The old company was grounded in that
German technique [The Rudolph von Laban-Mary Wigman-Hanya
Holm Technique which is the direct antecedent of Alwin Nikolais
and Murray Louis.] and it was choreographed in that technique. We
now are no longer trained in it and Murray isn't really interested in
choreographing in it either. He finds more nuance and more interest
in a hinted-at expression than in plotting out specific structure, as had

happened in *Calligraph for Martyrs* or *Bach Suite.* It's specific, visible structure and very solid, very valid.

Phyllis said that the choreography was explained to them from the premises of the German technique, like space, and that those words didn't mean the same to you now and therefore there was a different feeling to it. When you use the words "German technique" what exactly do you mean? Can you give an example of how it went?

The old technique was concerned with space. As we are. But the old technique *was* the spatial sense. You learned the spatial sense in class by defining strict spatial forms—circles in the air in front of you, above you, behind you, underneath you—which you could indicate with different parts of your body, or with directional looking with your eyes, or with an actual stepping of the feet on the floor, making a floor pattern. One example is scallops. You take three steps to make a half a circle on the floor as a floor pattern, then make a half turn, then go into the next half circle with three more steps. That was one kind.

Another kind would be what we call overcurves and undercurves. An overcurve in another technique would be called a leap: making the weight take off from one foot on the floor and landing on another foot, the pattern you make in space being like an arch. You curve over the space underneath you. You go up, you go over, you come down; that's what constitutes an overcurve. We would spend entire classes learning how to lift the thigh, extend the leg, point the toe to the place on the floor where we wanted to go, then go there. You would begin by just stepping, not really going into the air, not really doing the air work first—just lifting the thigh and extending the leg and stepping where you intended to go. So you were *aware* of where your leg was going and how it was going and the mechanics in lifting it.

Then on top of that would come the breath sense. The lift of the chest, the lift of the spine, your awareness of where the top of your head is in space as you go up and over, up and over. Then you would take it on and go a little faster and begin to do actual leaps up into the air and keep the same breath sense, the same top-of-the-head sensation, the same lift of the thigh and extending of the foot toward the spot on the floor where you're supposed to land.

Now you say, how is this different from a leap in a ballet idiom?

For ballet dancers, the classical grand jeté is a brushing through of the foot in plié, extending the leg very quickly and then lifting the entire leg up as the body is carried up and the other leg pushes you off the floor. So in a sense you have an extended leg and the rest of the body lifted together and pushed off the floor by the other leg, which is in plié. Then you reach the height of your curve, the extended leg in front tilts down, and you land on the foot that is in front of you. That's a leap.

But in what we call an overcurve, you really couldn't swing your leg through like that because it's not a spatial sense, it's a sense of the body, it's a way of pushing a leg through the space. What you see is extended leg and then the height to which it goes. My impression— and I've watched a lot of ballet and taken a lot of ballet—is that with a leap, ballet intends a spectacular height and a beautiful shape in the air. Not a going over, and a coming down, which our technique demands. All that is included in one overcurve.

The old technique went into this in minute detail and made sure that the student was aware of what his legs and his chest and his whole body were doing in relation to the space.

My impression is that the older technique comes down from a kind of German mentality that insists that abstract forms exist to be fulfilled and you bring yourself up to them. In our sense, perhaps, we create them more out of ourselves and more out of our *esprit*. The choreographer uses the dancer's energy in order to make the pattern, rather than insisting that the dancer correspond to already existing patterns.

In *Bach Suite* all those patterns already exist in the space, and we are there to demonstrate them to an audience, to make them aware that these patterns exist. This is now my interpretation of it. I don't know if everyone would agree. We surprise the audience by showing them things they didn't expect to see. We hope to delight them by manipulating them in pleasant ways, unexpected ways, illuminating ways. It's a lot of fun to do because it is a joyous dance and the feeling that we get from dancing it is one of joy. But those forms are there and they must be shown.

In a piece like *Porcelain Dialogues* there's nothing preexisting. We as individuals must create the atmosphere. We're helped by lights and slides and music, but if the dancer is a stick of wood up there on the stage, nothing happens, nothing is there. So we must create the poetic atmosphere in which the events happen. Forms are created and disappear. It's a great responsibility because you don't learn in class things that you can fall back on. You only know what Murray has told you in terms of the movements you have to do. Beyond that it's really up to the six people on stage to create a web of energy and of communication among them in order to make the work of art happen. Consequently I would imagine that it would be difficult to tape or to film *Porcelain Dialogues* because the thing that comes across to an audience, the thing that they grab hold of, is so impalpable, so imperceptible.

It's like gossamer.

Yes. It's not steps and not forms, it's an atmosphere.

Whereas Proximities *is different.*

Proximities has strong forms. A lot of symmetry, a lot of shapes that the dancers go into and come out of, and again (almost like *Bach Suite*) create the forms that are already there. Murray used freer forms for *Proximities* than he did for *Bach Suite*, but that was his own artistic evolution from 1958 to 1969. Also—this is another little thing—dancers in those days were a lot heavier than they are now. They could give a weight. When their bodies went hurtling through space, that was mass. It was a force of nature. In the film that we learned *Bach Suite* from, there's Gladys Bailin and Beverly Schmidt and a number of others. Not that they were fat, but they had heft. Maybe it was also psychic. They had authority about them that was grounded into them by Nikolais, by that Hanya Holm technique, and we haven't had that. It doesn't interest Murray to teach this technique to us either, because he's interested in his own exploration of energy and uses of energy in the body and outside the body coming out.

If he were in the old technique you'd all be different.

Absolutely.

I still think it was worthwhile to revive Bach Suite.

If it were possible to put the original company on the stage now at the age the members were then, they might get a few titters, because it's not the style of dance today nor has it the same passion.

After *Proximities* [1969] Murray started choreographing in a new way. He had a company of fine dancers who could follow his thoughts and his theorizing on ways of using energy and ways of performing which he had thought about during his own performing career, but which were not really possible within the context of the Nikolais pieces. So when Murray finally got his own company of very good dancers he could go on into areas of spatial and energy considerations that were not given much thought within the Nikolais theory.

Murray's whole concept of inner space and body textures was a use of energy which was not much touched on in the Nikolais technique—I guess it still isn't. Anyway, these new, subtle uses of energy resulted in choreography which depends *so much* on things that can't be talked about, or things which can't be said. There's no vocabulary for the way we dance. There's a nuance, you can see it and we can see it in each other and we can play with it ourselves and the audience can see it, but there's no verbal expression for it. Our dancers are now trained in this very subtle performing technique, and the old words which indicated a kind of movement to be done are not taught anymore and we're not used to doing it anymore. So *Proximities,* which was done that way, is very difficult *now* for the dancers to do.

How do you communicate the different qualities, the different principles of a piece? For instance, Continuum *is about time. How do you get someone to see what you want him to see?*

How do you make an audience see what you're talking about rather than what they expect to see? In a piece like *Continuum,* which has to do with time, people are not expecting to have to deal with time as a primary concept. Timing is always there but it's usually not noticeable as such. Well, in *Continuum* the way to deal with that is to have long stretches of seemingly nothing happening or things happening very slowly. That's the big clue for time. You see something happening very slowly when you would expect it to go much quicker. A dancer does a headstand, for example—he goes down on his head, puts his legs up in the air, then comes down again. Normally this could take maybe five seconds, but in *Continuum* it seems more like forty-five seconds, he does it so slowly. The fact that the piece is in slow motion is the first big clue to an audience. The problem with continuous slow motion is that the audience can get bored.

Well, Murray's device to keep them from getting restless is to make the shapes and the bodies and the lighting so ravishingly beautiful and sensual and sexy in a way, that the audience is kept watching, over the span of time that he wants them to, by the sheer beauty of what's going on on the stage. Then, after a period of watching this you may realize that slow motion, or perhaps the lack of big exciting things, is the point of the piece. That's a way of getting you to find out what the piece is about.

What do you think of when you perform Continuum?

Well, a dancer in our technique can be told that this is a piece about time and he will already have an idea of what you're talking about. You can teach *Continuum* to someone in about a half-hour rehearsal because you can teach the movements one right after the other, then say, "You do this until you hear the next music cue, then you go on to this, then you go on to that, and then you go on to that." It takes a short time to learn it and it seems like a short piece. But in performance with the tape it's all stretched out. You know your place in the time structure, principally by the music. You know when it's your turn to move, and the rest of the time you're holding still or very nearly still.

If you can listen to the music, wait for your music cue, do the thing that you have to do, and come to rest, you know that something's happening on the other side of the stage so you don't feel a great anxiety to keep the audience entertained. You can be comfortable with the fact that you know you're going to stand there for a while and the audience is not going to get bored. You have to have faith. You have to know that Murray has taken care of the design of the piece.

I would love to see *Continuum* because it has such a special feeling on stage. It is so strong, and there are certain performances when it takes over, catches you up in it, and is over before you realize it. *Continuum* always goes quickly for the performer because once you start, it's easy to be sucked right into it. Once it gets going it establishes its own pace, and you don't realize it's slow.

There's one section when we're all standing on one foot, and sometimes somebody falls over—that's all right, we've allowed for that

—but you suddenly realize you had to move your foot much too quickly to catch yourself, and that contrast makes you see how slowly you have been moving. The muscles remember how to move slowly, and once you get in that slowness it doesn't seem slow.

Let me go on to something like *Index. Index* is based on neuroses, so your thinking immediately changes. The idea of neuroses in the context of our piece is that there's little logic from one dance phrase to the next. Even as you're doing it, your head is pulled away from what you're doing. All through *Index,* except for maybe the finale, I keep my front brain away from what my body is doing, so you have almost a schizophrenia on stage. As Nikolais says, you're beside yourself—that is, the mind is not with the body, and that's how I perform the dance. My body goes ahead and does this thing almost obsessively; my mind is off someplace else. It's an interesting exercise. In order to perform some of the things you really do have to go back, pull it all together to make it happen, then pull right out again. Come to think of it, that really is creepy.

Index was choreographed very quickly. Then we had to learn how to perform it. Murray told us that it was about neuroses, and that it was to be done not detached, but unattached in the sense of being schizophrenic. Now, how do we get that across to the audience? Audiences are not dumb, they can see things happening. Everyone knows the cliché of the dance company with stone faces—the dancers who dance without a trace of expression. That in itself is schizophrenic, because the face is part of the whole being.

When audiences see these dance companies with the stone faces they know that something is wrong even if they don't know exactly what's wrong. Stone faces indicate to the audience that the whole being is not participating in the event. Whether the audience realizes it or not, that indicates a fracturing of the experience. It's not a whole experience; there's some secret being kept; something is going on underneath that they're not being told about. Poker faces. If you have a poker face you're keeping your hand to yourself, not giving any signals, and that's what communication between humans is.

Where does this fit in with Index?

In *Index* it's part of the choreography. Neurosis is not being with what you're doing. Murray was interested in the little neuroses of everyday life, like tapping your fingers on the desk top while you're

doing something else. It indicates that there's something else going on underneath that is suppressed or not being communicated. All of *Index* had that underneath, making the audience disturbed. It builds up to such a pitch that the final piece, the raga number, was designed as an outlet, a release of all that tension. To send an audience out into the night with a feeling of wanting to know more and not having it told to them is not nice to them. So the raga itself is really a very satisfying release of energy into space that rouses the audience and brings them quite up again. Even though we are still performing the raga without facial expression, the attack, the energy, is so expressive of release that it lets the audience release too. We can still maintain the frame-work of neurosis by keeping our faces passive.

I'd like to ask you one thing on a different subject. It's a long-standing debate among dance critics—whether the choreography or the performance comes first. Some people tend to put choreography first. I tend to put the performance first. It's rare to have the two equal.

Dance is a performing event. I think I enjoy a lot more dance than any of my friends do. Everyone goes and says, "It was ghastly, it was terrible." Phyllis Lamhut does the same as I do. She says, "I saw wonderful performances and lousy choreography, but I took it for what it was." I think that's the way I look at it too.

That's interesting because Phyllis was asking me why I had liked a Bolshoi performance of Sleeping Beauty, *when she hadn't enjoyed the performance much at all. I said that [Ludmilla] Semenyaka was marvelous and* Sleeping Beauty *is one of my favorite ballets, but I've never seen the performance of it that I want. For me, Semenyaka as Aurora was the whole evening, and everything else vanished completely. Because I'd seen a good Aurora, which doesn't happen very often, I was enthusiastic. Phyllis said that she thought the costumes were dreadful and she loved Semenyaka too, but not all the rest. For me, it didn't matter about all the rest. As far as I'm concerned, the things that move me are the ones that stand out.*

Energy expended upward may indicate aspiration *(Geometrics).* (Michael)

A calm shape moment in a whirlwind dance *(Glances).* (*l.* to *r.:* Anne-Robert, Helen-Michael, Bill, Dianne)

However, if you had been raised on Sleeping Beauties that had all the good qualities—good Aurora, good Bluebirds, good crowd staging, and so on, you would be very fussy. You are settling for the high spots and putting up with all the rest of it, which to our way of thinking is not what you should be doing. You should always have in mind the whole thing, but I think if you did, you would stop going to dance because so rarely does it happen that you have a perfect evening.

Something like *The Sleeping Beauty* or any other work of art is produced on levels of enjoyment. First of all, there's the splendor of the sets and the costumes and the music. You can bathe in the sensuous enjoyment of colors and lights and sounds. Then a very pretty girl comes on, and a handsome young man, and you can enjoy watching their athletic grace. Or you might enjoy lots of movement and favor the group numbers, or you might be a romantic and really get into the fairy tale, the story of a young girl who is enchanted. There are mythic reverberations to all that. Good triumphs over evil —there's that moral kind of satisfaction.

There's the skill of the choreographer, that within the tradition of western dance he has put together a satisfying, competent, workmanlike piece so that you get lyrical phrases or build to a climax and then pull away. There are these great dynamic hunks within a piece which you may or may not be aware of. If you are aware of them, you look for the phrasing of the whole thing. Like the Rose Adagio—well, you certainly are watching that girl to see if she's going to fall down. But then she triumphs in the end and she's standing there in attitude on point, and everyone claps and gets excited because she has triumphed. The choreographer has built into this thing a certain structure which leaves you satisfied when it happens. Then, I suppose, last of all is the actual performance moment. The moment when the artist brings the aesthetic into the audience's mind —the actual art experience—above and beyond the spectacle and skill. Does it all come together and happen as a spiritually satisfying event? With the audience's participation?

If you are experienced in watching dance, you are always hoping for the aesthetic triumph on stage as well as all the rest of it. Someone less sophisticated will be satisfied by the trappings which are the buttresses of the aesthetic vision. They are what shore up the final delicate thing. As in a cathedral, there's one set of columns that comes up to the top. They actually hold the thing up and make a statement on the aspiration of the architect. Then there's all this other stuff around—the stained glass windows, the spaces employed, the building materials and how it's carved, and how it all goes together.

I think if I had one more performance to go to in my life and had to choose between that particular Sleeping Beauty *and* Porcelain Dialogues, *I would take my chances and go to* Porcelain Dialogues.

Because there is a level of performance that always happens. Now you're responding to the total thing, which you would do with *Sleeping Beauty* too, if it happened totally all the time. It's easier for us because our company is so small and our artistic director is so strong. In the Bolshoi, you have all the dead wood sitting around drawing their pensions or about to draw their pensions. They're just waiting out the last couple of years until they can retire, which happens in State Opera ballets. The choreographers are obliged to use masses of people because it's spectacle and it's demanded in certain situations.

Do you think that picking out the high spots is a valid way to enjoy something?

It's not a question of validity, it's a question of necessity. I think that's the only way you can enjoy as collaborative a form as theater. When you have collaborations you usually have weak links and strong links, and you have to put up with it because there will always be the weak links. If you enjoy it, if you're willing to do it, of course it's valid. But I don't think that someone who has more rarified opinions, more rarified enjoyments, should be required to enjoy that same *Sleeping Beauty.* Maybe that's why it's good that we have variety so that everybody is happy.

I think a dance critic has an obligation to look at other things, to take everything into account. You can't just indulge yourself and take what you want out of it. Very often from a bad performance you learn what's good.

I don't think there's any professional stage performance that doesn't have some pleasure involved in the viewing of it. Really professional presentations always come up to a certain minimum. I find that even in quite amateur performances there are moments which are quite

lovely, quite unexpected, and they surprise you, take you off your guard.

If the choreography is good it sets up the performer wonderfully. That's why I've enjoyed dancing for Murray for so long, because I have utter trust in the choreography. We're not at all unsure whether it's good stuff that we're presenting. We have complete confidence in the material and so we're free to go on and invest as much of ourselves as our training, as our lives, allow us.

Isn't it practically impossible to dance for someone whose choreography you don't believe in?

If you have a steady job in dance—which is not that secure a profession—you'll stick with it. That's too bad but it's a fact—unless you get schizo. Then you have to leave, you have to change your life. But so much dance training is so bad that dancers don't realize that what they are doing is garbage—even if they are trained in New York, even if they are professionally trained.

I don't think anything in dance training prepares people to be an audience, to look at choreography, to know what's good and what's bad. I suppose if you live in New York you know that certain companies have great reputations and you go to see their stuff, and that may be what guides your taste. Still, it's not really an informed way of looking at it. It's like going to movies and seeing only the critically acclaimed films. Going to see only the critically acclaimed dance companies never lets you develop your own taste buds. You just accept someone else's ham and eggs.

Most of the young dancers I meet are all shopping. They are unconvinced about what they want to do, although they are all professional dancers. They take classes from different people and hope for instant success.

I'm afraid that's ninety-five percent of dance students. At Connecticut College a couple of years ago Murray looked around and said, "All

The weight directed away from the body's center generates motion (*Afternoon*). (*l. to r.:* Anne, Michael, Sara, Bill, Janis)

these kids are here expecting the word to be dropped on them." And he said that they are not going to get it because there are just so many individuals teaching classes and there's no Bible, there is no one way. You may be lucky enough to have a teacher who turns you in such a way that you find a direction, you know which way you're going. Then you can count yourself lucky, particularly if you're still a student. I was lucky that way. Everybody in our company was lucky that way.

But I think that's unusual.

Yes. Very unusual.

Chapter
six

The
audience
must not be
lulled

Choreography
Dancing within one Technique
Music

*Several weeks later the Murray Louis Dance
Company was in Philadelphia, where I joined them
for the weekend. We had decided to talk about
choreography and music in dance after watching a
performance of a dance choreographed to Bach's
music—a performance in which the use of music was
particularly thought-provoking. We were in the Ben
Franklin Hotel.*

I'd like to discuss choreography.

In our school everyone is encouraged to choreograph. As a matter of
fact when I went to the Playhouse back in 1966, Nikolais, Phyllis,
everybody got after me. I'd go to composition class for a while, then
I'd drop out, and I'd stay out. The next year, classes would start and
I'd go for a week or so and then drop out. Choreography is incredibly
hard work and I'm a lazy person, I have to admit.

In order to choreograph you have to have a certain craziness in
you. You choreograph because you *have* to, not because you want to
or because someone else wants you to. You choreograph because
there's that within you that cannot be expressed in any other way.
And my personal expression is in performing. I always thought it
wasn't realistic of modern dance training in general to put such heavy
emphasis on composition, because so few people will ever become
choreographers. However, Clive Barnes is currently bemoaning the

fact that there are so few really great classic choreographers that he counts them on the fingers of one hand.

Perhaps if there were more inculcation of the principles of composition and choreography in general dance training, more choreographers would come forth. If it's not taught to the general run of dance students, people don't feel they are expected to choreograph and they don't plumb their depths to find out if it's really within them. Well, I was encouraged to choreograph in class and it didn't interest me somehow. How can I say that? Because I have a feeling that if something is right for you it will happen and you'll do it, whatever the obstacles or whatever the situation.

In my case there was as much nurturing as I could possibly dream of if I had had the urge to be a choreographer, and it didn't happen. It hasn't happened yet because I feel fulfilled as a performer. I'm also awed at the amount of conviction, faith, and energy it takes to be a choreographer. You have to be convinced that what you have to say is worth saying in that medium. You have to have such faith in it that you would be willing to go through exhausting days and nights and weeks and months in order to accomplish it, and I don't feel that kind of compulsion. I *have* choreographed. I choreographed a couple of pieces when the Louis company put on a single performance of works by the dancers rather than by Murray. We did it because we had some time and some of the people wanted to do it. I choreographed a solo for myself and a trio for three other people. They were pleasant pieces, not challenging and not terribly thought-provoking, I suppose, but I enjoyed doing them because we had studio space, we had dancers available, and I had pleasant music to work with.

Who was in the trio?

Robert Small, Helen Kent, and Les Ditson. They were marvelous to work with. Having topflight dancers makes it so much easier because they do half the work themselves, and that's nice. It's harder to have to take raw students out of the school and infuse them with ideas or convince them as people that it's worthwhile to go into this, which is usually what happens when you're choreographing. You have to convince your dancers that it's worthwhile in order to ride on their enthusiasm, because it's a give-and-take situation: they have faith in you as a choreographer and you are sustained by their enthusiasm. If either of those things is missing it's pretty deadly.

I've never been able to verbalize well in terms of what I want in dance. I can look at what I've choreographed and say, it needs this and this and this. But to give images to the dancers so as to bring out that little extra something that polishes and makes another layer, perhaps, I find that very difficult. I did a couple of technically interesting pieces but I don't know how resonant with meaning they were. I don't know if I was *expected* to do anything that was resonant with meaning, but if you're going to be a choreographer you have to be concerned with meaning. There is the craft and there is the art. The craft can be learned, the art is already in you. You have to make a statement, and the point of it is what you pull out of yourself. The craft is what you can accumulate and work with. Also there are devices of choreography which you learn only by doing. You work within your medium. You learn shortcuts, things that seem to work in the way you want them to. This is true of any art, composition of music, anything. You learn effective combinations.

How to get everybody into a certain thing and how to get them out again.

Right. Devices of form. Certain forms work in certain expressive ways and certain other forms are completely wrong. In *Porcelain Dialogues,* Murray's Tchaikovsky piece, we dance in a circle—the oldest form of group dancing. After a sort of moving all over the stage we suddenly break into a circle, and I'm sure it's very satisfying suddenly to see a very simple form happen on the stage. Things like that you learn— when to use devices and when to avoid them. All this takes years.

Murray is expert because he's been choreographing for twenty-five or thirty years, both as a student and later on in his professional seasons. I don't think there is anybody working now who is more of a craftsman than Murray. With his craft and his knowledge he can say anything he wants to say. And consequently the work is important, because the more sophisticated your knowledge, the more subtly you can get at states of feeling, states of being, comments about humanity. Whatever you're trying to say you can refine and refine until you gorge an audience on richness.

A kid in college will choreograph a dance about the joy of spring and it's nice to see, but it's naïve. Murray has choreographed a dance [*Proximities*] about joy, about people being close to each other, but it's done in a sophisticated way, on many levels. There are many levels of pleasure in being next to each other in that piece. Then you get to his big resonant theater pieces like *Index* and *Scheherazade*.

They clang through your head with images; they draw people out of themselves; they wreck you. You come out of the theater with your eyes crossed. It takes years and years to achieve that. Maybe I'm intimidated because I work with such a fine choreographer, but at the same time I don't resent being in the presence of a master.

Murray said that you should choreograph every day.

That's the philosophy of the school. I suppose writers say that too. I read Ray Bradbury once on writing. He said, "Write every day, even if you're not going to use it. Write a thousand words a day." I suppose if you composed a phrase a day you would begin to be selective about what you like and what was working and what was not. Very valuable. Again you have to have the compulsion. Murray doesn't need choreographers for his performers although I think people with choreographic ability probably are better performers.

Why?

Because they are wittier. They have an insight into the work which just a hoofer wouldn't have. You know what I mean by hoofer? Someone who just does the steps.

Do you think that's necessarily true? I'm not sure.

If you're working in art dance, a creative outlook will help you a great deal, I think. Of course it's possible for performers who have never even thought of choreographing, or don't want to, to do very sensitive, deep things. Perhaps it comes out of their own intuition, or perhaps the choreographer has led them along such a path that they will go into the right thing almost without being told. It probably happens most of the time with fine dancers who haven't any choreographic experience. Great dancers have that creative component in their performance skill even if they don't want to be choreographers, even if it never occurred to them to be choreographers.

Do you think your viewpoint might change?

Oh, if someday it changes, that's fine with me. I don't anticipate it.

I'm just going to let the future happen.

*Change of subject. Earlier you talked about how narrow-minded some
dancers are about ways of doing things, yet in a way you're doing the
same thing. Are you narrow-minded?*

I'm narrow-minded in the sense that I've been brought up in a
certain discipline, a certain philosophy about movement. The space,
time, shape, motion, energy structure of the philosophy guides my
thinking.

*But doesn't it have to be that way? Isn't it one of the characteristics of
modern dance that everybody has a point of view?*

Right. The point of view has to be strongly emphasized.

How do you get around that? Or do you want to get around it?

I don't think it's necessary to get around it if you have a composer
like Murray who is prolific enough and whose ideas are of enough
substance. It's not necessary for performers to stretch their brains
beyond that umbrella under which it is all happening.

*But you also said it's like not opening your mind up to different ways
of doing things.*

When I go to the theater or the movies or things like that, I enjoy
lots of different things. I try to find out the atmosphere of what is
going on, which is usually revealed as soon as the curtain goes up.
After you find out the atmosphere there are clues as to what the
choreographer or the movie maker or the dramatist is trying to get at.
Then maybe a third of the way into the piece you say, I think I can
follow this path. Or if you are narrow-minded or close-minded you
bang down the curtain and you're not going to learn anything; it's a
dead end.

*Do you have to have a great deal of confidence before you can look at
some completely different way of dancing?*

I think so, because you feel threatened if you are observing a rival
take over the stage and manipulate an audience. But I go to be
manipulated. I love to go to the theater and have my insides smushed
around by whatever's happening on stage. I think that's great. That's
what theater's for. If you go with an attitude that what you yourself

do on stage is art but what you see others do is not art, you're being pompous and letting yourself miss out on a lot of rich experiences.

Now I must editorialize for a moment. A lot of the stuff you see is crap. In a lot of dances there are moments which are really beautiful or poetic or startling—and they resonate in the mind—but then all the rest of the piece drags it down. Or, on the other hand, you watch a lot of dreariness and suddenly when you see something good it stands out like a jewel. Sometimes that's a trick, I'm sure. Some choreographers crank out steps and then, whether by preordination or happy accident, something really original or really nice happens. And then they work around that and make that the point. To me that seems like cheating, it's not treating the audience with respect. It's just doing your own thing for catharsis or exhibitionism or whatever your motivations are.

Let's talk about living within one technique. The big techniques that are around are very powerful and seductive.

Because they are shaped in one idea and each is a product of one person's mind. You don't make art by committee, so when one person's concept guides the whole thing you get a certain richness, a certain differentness. As soon as you bring in more people, it begins to level out and everyone is pleased or everyone is displeased. Murray, while he doesn't actually design the costumes, has the okay on them. It's not that somebody upstairs says, "Fred is going to design the costumes and Murray is going to do the choreography," as they did in the Diaghilev ballet. Diaghilev chose a scenarist and a choreographer, one who said what was going to happen and another who gave the steps, showing what was going to happen. I was astonished when I read that because I'm used to thinking of choreographers as the pivotal point around which the whole thing revolves.

It seems to me that with one kind of technique you could live your whole life without ever questioning it and just be cradled in it, or live in a cocoon.

That's all right for a performer within that technique but for a critic, no.

I'm not talking about myself.

I know, but you're seeing it from the critic's point of view. You have

see a lot of things and you have to try to understand many points
f view. If you're performing within one technique, that technique is
l you really have to know. Where that leads depends upon the
rtility of the technique. If you're stuck in a sterile, step-oriented
chnique, that's the kind of dancer you'll be, and you will probably
nd up unhappy because you're not fulfilled and you don't know
hat's wrong. A lot of dancers break away from their choreographers
ecause they feel that there's no chance for personal expression and
ıey're not getting the richness that they should. I don't feel that
ith Murray's choreography. Maybe if I danced in it another ten
ears I would.

Ballet dancers have to change their style from modern to classical
ke *Sea Shadow* to *Raymonda*. I don't know of any modern dance
ompany that has to make similarly jarring style changes from piece to
iece. It must be very difficult for a ballet dancer. So much depends
n the artistic director.

*ı other words, somebody can remain encapsulated in one modern
yle?*

es, I think so, and still contribute their own personal richness to the
ork, and be fulfilled at the same time. I suppose it depends on how
ır-ranging the person is who works within that technique. Now,
eople like Murray or Nikolais, who are originators and pioneers
ithin the field, they almost have to close themselves off from other
ıfluences. Murray doesn't do it so much, but Nikolais rarely goes to
ıe theater, never goes to dance if he can help it, rarely goes to films
ecause what he has boiling within him is so endlessly fascinating to
im that he is satisfied just to be having that gestating within him all
ıe time. And that's all right. Murray likes to go out and see some
allet and some films. He loves movies. He doesn't see as many as he
ould like to.

Murray likes classical music. Nikolais really can't stand any music
—well very little anyway, because he has his own kind of vision about
ɔund and sound's function and music's function. What makes his
ance theater unique is that strong vision. But his dancers don't have
ɔ have the conviction—that this is the only way. They can be
clectic in their own tastes, in their own satisfactions.

ː always surprises me when dancers walk out of a concert, any dance concert, and say they can't stand to see any more of that kind of movement.

They probably won't put up with the low points in order to get to the high points, which I will a lot of times. I'll put up with the long, boring stretch in order to get to the good points at the end. Maybe they are talking about the attitude of the dancers instead of the movements. For instance, to anyone from our technique an emotional veneer which is laid over a whole piece is offensive because we're taught to be so careful of emotional veneers. We are a little leery about a dramatic element rather than a motional or pure dance element. Anything is valid if it's integral and true to itself. But if an emotional layering gets smeared over every piece in the repertory, or changes only slightly from piece to piece, that's a performing mannerism which is not valid unless the choreographer wants it for his whole body of work.

The choreographer has to be very careful as an artistic director. He has to tell the dancers what he wants in terms of images or in terms of emotion. Then the same choreographer will go ahead with what he thinks of as a completely abstract piece and it doesn't work because the dancers layer it with a dramatic thing that the audience can't figure out because there has been no such intent in the choreographer's mind. Sometimes the choreographer will be blinded to the layering and he'll say he didn't intend it as having any great dramatic qualities. And yet the audience is confused because there are dramatic signposts in the performances.

For example, the way a dancer uses his head and his face is particularly symbolic, particularly significant in that sense. A straight-on face is fairly neutral. As soon as the head is tilted slightly to one side something else is being said. If the chin is tilted up and the gaze goes down the nose, there's a certain hauteur or regality involved. The dancer should be aware of all these little symbolisms of gesture, yet often he is not because the teachers and choreographers

Attentiveness is a necessary ingredient in the state of performance *(Porcelain Dialogues).* *(l. to r.:* Sara, Michael, Helen)

Six bodies make one shape for the stage picture *(Porcelain Dialogues).* *(l. to r.:* Sara, Anne, Robert, Helen, Michael, Jerry)

don't even tell him what his gestures are conveying to the audience. The dancer needs to be made aware of what he is doing.

If you're working with a lot of people, the structuring problems are so great that they tend to divert your real aesthetic drive. It's like handling traffic. Masses of people going from one side to the other will divert the choreographer, the director, the stager, the person who is putting it together, divert them so much that they may even forget their original aim. And that's too bad. I know I enjoyed putting together the couple of things that I've choreographed in the last ten years. But then Murray or someone would look at it and say: "There's a nice dance in there, but you have to sort it out and find out what it's really about." It was valuable because even I could see what grabbed the eye, but I could also see that an idea that I had imposed upon it from the outside, an idea that had snuck in in the process of construction, only confused the eye and watered down the dance.

How do you keep the ideas from sneaking in?

It takes a strong will, because sometimes the little sidetrack is simply charming and you don't want to get rid of it and then you have to ask, "Is this something that has to do with what I'm trying to say?" You have to be strong and save it for another time. A lot of choreographers won't do that. They'll keep in what they like, and it does not make for a strong stage statement. I should think that's what a choreographer would be after.

It's very easy to be facile.

Oh yes. For sure—particularly for Murray, who is so prolific. Innovation pours out of him; he rarely repeats a piece, his phrases or steps. Even if he does repeat, he's aware of it because we don't let him forget it. We say "That's from *Chimera*" or "That's from *Porcelain,* remember that?" And he says, "Well, now you do it with a different point of view," and then it becomes different. He has to watch himself to see that he isn't getting diverted from what he has to say. He's very good about that. He can watch and actually see what he's done, whereas a lot of creators will watch and see what they want to see, or see what they think they've done, rather than what is actually there in front of them. It's very difficult to see what's really there. The eye plays tricks.

*I'd like to talk about music also—the uses of music in choreography
and the way a performer uses music.*

Well, let's take the example of the dance concert we saw last week,
where one of the works was set to Bach. The convention of baroque
composers was that each section of the music had one mood or
feeling about it. When they had said all they wanted to say about
that, they went on to the next section in a different time signature
and a different key. That was because of the limitations of the
baroque orchestra.

Well, nowadays if you choreograph a piece with one dynamic or
mood per section, it's what we used to call Mickey Mousing the
music, or saying with the dancing the same thing that the music is
saying. The question arises: Why bother? As an audience you not only
ask the question but also go to sleep, because it gets very dull.

This particular piece we watched set to Bach, had a long, long
adagio. A great deal was happening in the dance on stage, but all the
movements had a similar dynamic attack, even so diverse a thing as a
pas de deux lying on the ground making shape things—from shape to
shape with a certain kind of energy thrust to them—and a getting up
and running around the stage while something else happened. The
running and the lying down were done with the same energy attack,
and it was long and seemed longer because there was no variation
within the dynamics of it. The music was going along on one
dynamic as well. So the whole audience sat back, and everyone was
beginning to cough and shuffle because the dance had the same
approach from phrase to phrase, from big chunk to big chunk,
through this long adagio.

It became predictable, and Murray says as soon as the audience
knows what to expect it loses interest. I suppose that's just a
condition of Western art. In the East it's not at all that way; they go
on for hours and hours within one framework; but in our Western
theater it's not that way. So if you are a choreographer, you have to
watch out when you're using a long piece of music—particularly
baroque music, which has this carry-through. You have to be careful
not to Mickey Mouse the music. It's very easy to do it without
realizing it, because the music tends to permeate the atmosphere and
you do not hear it or do not realize that it's blanketing what you're
doing. Unless you are very strong and insist upon new attacks and
fresh approaches within the dance structure, it will all even out and

get very much the same. I'm talking not so much about spectacle but about the middle of pieces when the audience sits back and wonders what's going to happen next.

As I say, the music permeates the atmosphere, and once the performer has learned the movements, the muscles themselves remember the movements—we call it muscle memory. If the performer is not always on top of what he's doing he can let his muscles do the movements; the music lulls him into this kind of dynamic sameness, and it becomes dull—even when the choreography is not meant that way. We can do that in our repertory in *Porcelain Dialogues* because the music is syrupy, with the violins and so on, and we can be listening to the music and enjoying it no end, forgetting our duty as performers to make a new vision out of what's being presented on stage rather than just dittoing the music. With Tchaikovsky that's dangerous because it's sweet music and it has a melody you can hum when you go out of the theater. It's almost our duty to shake up the audience and not let them fall into that. Murray always tells us to get on top of the music and not let the music get on top of us.

By being on top of the music he means a couple of things. One is that you have to anticipate what the music is going to do, whether it's lulling or exciting, and then you have to plan your dynamic strategy. How will I go into the next phrase? How will I attack it in order to make the audience see something fresh rather than what the music leads them to expect? Oftentimes, modern dancers and choreographers say that they are deliberately going against the music. But it isn't that so much. They're trying to do what I'm describing, but probably going against the music is the wrong way to say it. Sometimes I suppose it is jarring against the music. It probably shouldn't be jarring either, if you care to have your audience with you rather than outraged.

What does going against the music mean?

There are two ways of going against the music. You can outrage the audience by doing something unexpected or even offensive to them in relation to the music, or you can do what we try to do—keep the audience's eye fresh while it is listening to music which may be familiar, like Tchaikovsky or Brahms or Rimsky-Korsakov. Try not to let the audience expect the next thing. Perhaps to go against the

usic is simply not to follow it sheeplike, but to add a dimension to
to comment on it. Now I'm getting dangerously close to making
e music too important. We are discussing music. If I were
scussing dance I would say that probably the music shouldn't be a
mment on the dance or modify the dance, but I'm speaking of how
performer or a choreographer has to think about the music,
rticularly familiar music.

In the case of Nikolais's pieces he chooses to create his own
usic, to create an unfamiliar sound atmosphere so that the audience
n never be lulled because they have no idea what to expect from
e sound. When you are watching the dance and not even
rticularly listening to the sound or aware of the music, the
orations are disturbed in an unfamiliar way. Murray, being the
mantic that he is, chooses more familiar music. Although often he'd
e to have Nikolais scores for his pieces, Nikolais rarely has the time
do them.

en Nikolais scores turn into music after a while.

at's because Nikolais is a musician.

*u can go out humming some of his pieces. Does that have the same
d of danger then?*

ss danger because the harmonic structure is not familiar and he
vays messes up the rhythmic structure. For a while you can tap your
ot, but then the rhythm changes. We just got new finale music for
ometrics* and it has a very definite beat in it, but there are sections
ere heavy syncopation comes in. We're strapped there on stage
ing to hear the beat. To an audience it's enough to put an edge on
expectations. The audience is not lulled by knowing what to
ect.

w do you keep yourself shaken up?

our company, Murray has to do it. If you do the same piece time
er time, things happen to you without your even noticing it. Then
rray will step in and say: "Dolls, it's time to think a little more
out your phrasing in this piece." Or he'll watch from the wings and
ll say, "I don't know why that's not working tonight," and it'll
turb him. Then he'll think about it, and of course any number of
ngs will seem to be not going right. A lot of times it can be traced

back to dynamic energy attacks. How to go into each phrase freshly and to keep the audience's eye open and keep our heads open.

What do you have to do?

You have to keep your head working, as well as your body, as well as your muscles. Every performance. You can rely on your muscle memory to carry you through much of your performance on the stage while you're thinking about other things—staging or timing or things like that. The muscles remember the dynamics too.

But the muscles tend to let the energy levels become comfortable. At times you can do movement as expected within the requirements of the piece, and it's comfortable movement. At other times you must really break out of yourself and make yourself uncomfortable in order to speak with the piece, and that's what the muscles don't want to do. They don't want to go beyond their comfort zone, as Murray calls it. So they pull in a little bit each performance toward that comfort zone, and finally there you are riding through the piece as though you were sitting in an armchair. That's when the audience will sit back.

To a lay person it seems like a tremendous amount of energy being put out, but dancers are used to putting out that kind of energy. So you find your comfort within that great output, but it doesn't stretch you, it doesn't pull you out longer than you really are, it doesn't make you whip faster than you usually do. You really have to apply your mind to those things, particularly to beginnings. If you can attack a thing with a good clear attack the rest of the phrase— whether two counts or twenty-seven counts—will probably take care of itself because muscles are jarred into the level of perception that you want to get them to.

Is it a matter of individual dynamics or group dynamics?

Well, as performers you have to be responsible for your own movement first. But you also have to be on the lookout for everyone else as well. That's probably why it's so difficult. If you keep yours nice and safe, and if everyone else is doing the same thing, it will mesh together. That's when Murray accuses us of starting to be pretty, when everyone is loving it and it comes down to a lowest common denominator.

He uses the word monochromatic.

Exactly. That's the word for the Bach piece we saw the other night,
especially in the adagio sections. Monochromatic. Of course,
monochromaticity has its value. If you have done a very exciting
section, the audience needs a rest; then you need to pull it down. But
as a performer you have to be aware that now is the resting time, the
pulling away time, the lower energy time. You have to have the rests
between the exciting parts, and then you can build again. But you
have to be aware all the time of how it is happening.

I saw a dancer in another company perform a solo beautifully.
The movement was interesting and was done with great technical
expertise. But she accomplished it all with the view of doing it well,
of performing it beautifully, and thereby she lent a gloss to the whole
thing. In other words, her energies were in the service of making
beautiful movement rather than in the service of making the
movements pungent, changing the textures of the dance. It's like
putting varnish on an old painting, thus lending a lovely surface to it
—and maybe tinting all the colors in it to a certain range of tones
which make it soothing to look at, whereas perhaps the artist intended
that you be a bit disturbed by the blue down in the corner.

Just so, perhaps there should be disturbing elements within the
choreography. To gloss over, to make all the movement beautiful is
another trap. The dance becomes expectable and dull.

At the end of this dancer's solo there was great applause because
technically it was done very well and it was difficult to do and it was
pulled off. But no risks had been taken. Difficult movement, yes. But
there was no danger, no breathlessness to it. We knew it was going to
come out all right. It was beautiful but dull.

Sometimes there are whole companies built on beautiful
movement, and choreographers can be so seduced by it themselves
that they say, "That's the way I want it done." They don't realize
that in the rehearsal hall it looks fine but when you get a full evening
of it in a concert hall it palls pretty quickly because the audience's
appetite for variety is voracious.

*Shall we get back to music? Talk about it in terms of some of the
works—for instance,* Proximities *or* Bach Suite.

Bach Suite *has dangers in the music. The second Brandenburg
Concerto is exceptional because it has a lot of bright sound in it. The*

high trumpet, the underpinnings, the rhythm, the ground base in the background (whatever they call it) has an up feeling to it—Murray likes music with an up feeling rather than soothing music—and it is fast. We don't use the middle movement; we switched gears and took a gavotte from one of the Orchestral Suites because the middle movement of the Brandenburg has a definite melody and a long violin line which is soothing rather than exciting. Murray put in something a little more bumptious because the piece was short enough and didn't need a soothing section. He kept the whole piece pretty much in character—flashing attacks and dynamic variations within a more exciting high-energy range—rather than letting it soothe you and calm you for a while.

Proximities is German romantic music [the Brahms Serenade in A]. Certain composers shouldn't be used for dance, like Brahms in his later years. The Serenade is an early work of Brahms before his music got so heavy. It's quite delightful and seems like a light piece. You have to be careful what music you use. In *Scheherazade* Murray went through the tortures of the damned about whether to use the Rimsky-Korsakov. He went ahead and choreographed it to the Rimsky-Korsakov, but to put that on the stage with all the color and the texture and the variety within that music is to take the chance of having the audience just listen to it and not watch what's going on.

So what do you as the dancer have to do? If you're going to perform Porcelain Dialogues [*Tchaikovsky*], *what do you think about?*

Just before the performance I really have to pull my head together because I can be shattered by anyone's lack of concentration. I don't think so much about what I'm going to do as about the general atmosphere of the piece. It has to be delicate, it has to be quiet, and yet as each person gets up to do his thing it has to be a new sentence about a new subject with someone new speaking. Robert Small starts it, he sets a mood, and other things happen out of that. You have to watch from section to section, particularly if you have the next solo coming up.

Defining space out beyond the fingertips *(Porcelain Dialogues).* (*l. to r.:* Sara, Jerry, Michael [leaping], Robert, Helen)

Energy is used purely in the service of the motional excitement *(Porcelain Dialogues).* (*l. to r.:* Jerry, Sara, Helen, Michael, Anne, Robert)

Does this affect how you do yours?

Sure. We can pretty much know what's going on with each person's variations. Mine, I must say, change drastically from performance to performance. There are chancy balances and turns and things which sometimes work in a spectacular way and sometimes work in other ways. Sometimes I fall down, much to my horror. But you go on from there and try to pull something constructive out of the ashes.

How about something like Moments, *where the men are all doing exactly the same thing?*

That's constructed on the principle of soloist and corps, and as a part of the corps you really don't have to do a lot of pondering how to go into it. All four of the corps men are considered as a unit, and we can almost ignore the way Murray plays this role and always be constant in what we do in order to provide a ground so that he can take off from that. And he does. He hasn't performed it twice the same way since he's been doing it because he's still experimenting with the solo role. So we try to be very steady. With Nureyev that was easy because he's so steady himself. In fact I think he was rather pleased that that's the way it happened because I'm sure he doesn't want unexpected, distracting things coming out of his corps.

Moments *is not really built to have unexpected, distracting things.*

Right, except for the soloist. But that's okay. It gives you a rest between two other pieces on a program.

If you're in a piece like that, in a corps like that, you can't go to sleep.

No. But our movement is not choreographed in relation to the music at all, really. Long music phrases bound our dance phrases, but that's about it, except for one little quick section in the middle when we really do dance on the beat, when Murray is upstage, his back to the audience. But it's such a minor part of the piece, that little section where the corps is really dancing, it is in such contrast with the rest of the role that the dancer can't fall asleep doing it.

What is a dance phrase?

It's like a music phrase. It can be any length of time from the beginning of one gesture going through a series of gestures and ending with a gesture or a movement.

But does it have to do with the music or with the dance?

If you're choreographing beat for beat with the music, it'll tend to go
with the music. It's completely analogous to the music phrase. In
music notation there would be long arcing curves over the entire
length of the phrase, and that's almost there in the dance phrase as
well. There can be many movements in a dance phrase, just as there
can be many notes in a music phrase, but they all tend to belong to
one section. Then they reach a conclusion or a stopping place and
something new takes over.

   The phrases are the building blocks of the structure. You can
have short choppy phrases and build to great excitement or you can
have long, singing, melodious phrases which are beautiful to see.
Murray likes long dance phrases. He chose the Brahms that we use
because it has long phrases. The first phrase is nineteen counts long,
which is a good length for a phrase.

   If he's choreographing rhythmically to a beat when we don't
have a score yet we'll always tend to go into sixes rather than fours.
We'll do a six-count measure because it isn't an expectable form and
yet it doesn't become unmanageable. All of *Landscapes,* the finale of
Index, all are in sixes.

   Now that's not to say that we don't throw in an eight here and a
two there, and so on. But Murray feels good about a six measure. And
then there will be maybe four measures of six, six measures of six in a
phrase, a longer phrase, and the phrases add up into a longer
structure. That's how Murray builds his pieces, architecturally. By
measure, by phrase, by overall structure. He watches the dynamics
very closely because he knows what an audience needs and wants.
He's concerned that the audience gets its satisfaction.

In Proximities *did he begin with the music or did he put the music on
after he had planned the dance?*

He knew what he wanted to do with his dance, and he was looking
around feverishly for music. One day he heard this on the radio and
said: "That's my music." Then he got the recording and brought it to
the studio, and we listened to the pulse. He doesn't play the music a
lot when he's composing. He tends to play the music once and get an

idea of tempo and length of phrase or length of major phrases. Then he'll go ahead and choreograph the sixty-four counts or whatever, then play the music while the dancers run through it to see if any chopping or cutting has to be done to fit the music. But he tries not to let the music affect him note for note.

In *Proximities* there is a lot of running over the music phrases. The dance phrases run right through the music phrases or just miss the music phrases, and it was originally difficult to learn the music. Because there are a lot of rhythmic subtleties in Brahms's score and we did not pay attention to them, mistakes cropped up here and there and we didn't know what was wrong. We really had to analyse the score. Murray tends not to do that, so we had to do it for ourselves.

Why is Proximities *so hard?*

First of all the music is very complex, at least in terms of the dancer's beat, by which I mean a very even beat. Well, Brahms was free to use any kind of syncopation or coloration or rubato in order musically to do his thing, and so we have to know what he was doing.

Our second movement and Brahms's second movement are almost two different things, because Brahms composed it in a very fast, syncopated three-eight time and our second movement is in three-four time. Now, you may think there wouldn't be any problems. But one of our measures is worth two of his, and his beat comes on the "one" of each of his measures, which comes on the "one" and the "and" of the "two" of one of our measures. But he's also syncopating within his measures. If you just listen to the music you might think that it goes, "and-a-one-and-a-two-and-a-three, and-a-one-and-a-two-and-a-three." But if you look at the music on the page that's not what he's doing. That's the pulse you hear, but it's not the pulse of the written score. If you ever see someone conducting that score, notice that the baton is not going anything like what the dancer's feet are stepping. It's a crazy, crazy syncopation, and every once in a while in the second movement, leftover beats accrue and Brahms has to do a transition where everything evens out and he can start fresh again. But the dancers are left with a few three-eighth notes extra and don't know what to do with them because there's no choreography. So we just glide over them and grit

our teeth and prepare for the next phrase. With tape music it's fairly
possible because you know when to expect the unexpected.

That's one of the difficulties. Someone learning *Proximities* has a
horrible struggle to hear a lot of the phrasing in the music. We do
most of it merely by phrase instead of by beat, by pulse, so they have
to be able to hear the phrasing. Brahms's phrasing is beautiful and
subtle, and a lot of our phrasing depends on hearing his beginnings or
his endings and then knowing how to go on to the next thing, which
is difficult for someone learning the piece. Also, the choreography
itself is difficult—it was the last piece to be choreographed in the old
Nikolais technique, the old German style. *Proximities* was
choreographed within that milieu, and in those days the dancers on
whom it was choreographed knew what was expected and did it.

As new people came into the company, all we could do was
teach them the movement and give them the sense of the whole
piece, which is the enjoyment of it and the strong phrasing of the
music, and tell them how to do the movement. In other words, it was
almost like teaching them the specific technique for doing that piece.
So from dancer to dancer it's handed on, with me there for the whole
time. There are many reasons why *Proximities* is the most difficult in
our repertory for the performer.

Now, what we have been talking about is fairly subtle stuff for
the audience. Music is a big clue because we've all been raised on it.
Music is a strong, unconscious stimulator. It can be happening to you
without your being directly aware of it. Music flavors the atmosphere
in which the dancers move and in which the piece takes place. If you
want an atmosphere of Russian soul, you use the Tchaikovsky quartet.
If you want a ratata shake-it-up atmosphere you might use what we
use in the finale of *Geometrics* by Nikolais—unfamiliar music but
with energy drive.

The audience responds very strongly to music. In making a
program for the evening you have to be concerned about what the
music is. We wanted to take *Porcelain Dialogues* [Tchaikovsky],
Moments [Ravel], and *Index* [Oregon Ensemble], but we couldn't
take *Porcelain Dialogues* and *Moments* together because that would
be two string quartets in a row and it would pall on an audience. We
try not to put two electronic scores together because it makes an
audience uncomfortable, or if we do, they have to be dissimilar in

character. *Facets* [Nikolais] and *Chimera* [Nikolais] had that problem when we did them in New York. They were on the same program back to back, and it was disturbing to some people. They said we really should start the program with *Facets,* then do *Bach Suite,* then do *Chimera* because we would have the Bach between two electronic scores.

I didn't notice it at all.

There was an intermission between the two. Also you may have seen them enough so that you are not listening to the music and you're just watching the performance so strongly that you are less affected by the music than someone seeing the dances for the first time. Almost all the reviews mention the music of *Chimera* as being important to it and it is. It's a strong, lovely score as opposed to *Facets,* which is almost background music. It's concrète—that is to say, it's real sound rearranged, whereas *Chimera* is electronic. Now we have *Geometrics* [electronic], *Moments* [string quartet], and *Index,* which is an improvised instrumental score—very beautiful. [This was the program given at the Walnut Street Theater in Philadelphia.]

It certainly is interesting to see the difference between the two Nikolais scores in the ending of Geometrics.

Yes. We were thinking of having *Geometrics* end the program but the singing score we had before was not strong enough. It was lovely music and a joy to dance to. But it lent to that finale a long phrase, singing, musical look. Now that there's this really high-powered score the steps are still the same and the concept is still the same but the audience carries away more of a hard, dynamic feeling and we dance it differently. It's much faster than it used to be. We have to make it smaller and punchier now in order to do the steps. It has been forced to change. The more we do it, the more comfortable it feels and it started to feel really good just in terms of its being faster, although at first that new score was such a trauma.

Why?

A witty moment from *Schubert.* (Anne, Michael)

We had to go over it seventeen times on a performance day. Nikolais just gave it to us and stood and counted it at us while we were dancing. It was terrible. Also it's composed in eights, and our dance was counted in threes.

What did you do?

Some phrase beginnings in the music correspond with phrase beginnings in the dance, so you can pick it up sometimes. You just learn when you have to ignore the big accents in the music and when you can take those cues. The nice thing about tape music as opposed to an orchestra is that it's always the same, you can anticipate it.

What about dancing with an orchestra?

It's very exciting, a very different feeling. To have someone in the pit there warming up while you're coming into the theater lends much more excitement than just seeing two dead speakers with no sound coming out. However, once the performance has started, I think tape is as good as an orchestra. I don't know how a performer who usually dances to an orchestra would answer this. But to us, who usually dance with tape, it is interesting to change off to an orchestra every now and then because you always have that unknown element—are they going to mess up or not? It's nice for us for a change, but I certainly would rather dance to tape than an orchestra. It's dependable. Even at that, the current varies from place to place, and the tempo of the tape varies. We carry a variable speed tape deck so we can choose our own tempo for pieces, and that's a real luxury. For certain pieces it makes a lot of difference; for other pieces it doesn't matter at all. *Hoopla* can be done at any tempo. *Proximities* is touchy; we like to have that at a very specific tempo.

Chapter
seven

*Everyone
has to come to
terms with what they
have to give*

Conclusion: two and a half years later
changes

*Time passes, people change. Michael and I met in
my apartment in New York two and a half years after
our last conversation to talk once more.*

*I'd like to talk about the changes that have happened since our last
conversation of two and a half years ago. For instance, from the time I
first met you, the company members have changed. Only you and Anne
[McLeod] and Robert [Small] are still there. Does it make a big
difference when somebody leaves?*

Oh yes. There have been big changes. Marcia [Wardell] was the first
to go. She had such an incredible performing range and technique
and was such a beautiful figure on stage that it was a dreadful loss.
Richard Haisma left. Richard was very intellectual and it was difficult
for him to work into the intuitive, spontaneous working conditions
that we have, but eventually he did it very well. He was a wonderful
performer, but his choreographic urges got too strong for him and he
had to leave and work on his own.

Probably the biggest change occurred when Helen Kent left to
be on her own to choreograph for herself. From the day she joined in
1970 she made a family atmosphere for the company which was
extraordinarily strong. She was wonderful in that she always listened
to what each person had to say. She was very involved personally with
everyone in the company, and she was also a strong performer. When
she left the fabric of the company became a little looser. Not that
that's bad, but the sense of family is not as strong as it was. Annie
and Robert and I are a little cooler in that sense, and not so
personally involved with everyone in the company. Helen was a nexus
and all the relationships went through her.

The company now feels very young. This is all right—the sense of youth is very good—I like that. The new members have a lot to work on, but they all have wonderful qualities which are coming out.

Has the look of the company changed?

In terms of the company look changing, it struck me that three years ago I talked about how we dance on the balls of our feet rather than using a hard toe—in other words, the balls of the feet received the weight which made a softer look to our dancing. I think this was true up to 1976. Murray has gradually begun to be more concerned with a spectacular technique. Now, that's not in terms of circus show-off, but he wants a sense of great facility in his dancers. He wants the extended foot. We still put the weight on the ball of the foot but as soon as the foot comes off the floor he wants a very extended foot and knees straight in the air. He wants brilliant leg work—he actually used that phrase.

This may be because—and this is my conjecture—the company changed and Bill Holahan came to us. Bill comes from a background of Graham and ballet where there is a strong emphasis on brilliant technique, and he brought that to his roles. Murray saw it and he liked it. We found ourselves being criticized with phrases like—"Bill does this movement in a particular way. I would like you to watch and see how he does it." Bill has an incredible energy attack. He commands attention not only because he is so tall but because his energy is on the surface and so available. Murray saw it and he liked it. This does not change anything in terms of the basic thought about the technique—it's just a way of going about it.

Bill is the first person to come into the company from another technique.

New blood, new thought comes in. But I really want to stress that the theory has not changed. In dance there are any number of emphases you can place in any number of areas.

Come to think of it, Robert has for years been developing the same kind of spectacular style, but from inside the technique, from his own nerve responses and energy releases. Murray has always been interested in energy and the use of energy and the attack into the movement, and when he saw Robert and then Bill doing it he liked it very much. We all have it in us I think; it's just acquiring a shift of thought of how you go about it.

I mentioned in the old days when *Proximities* was choreographed, it was softer and more romantic. Then we began to add more attack to it—a flashing, darting quality—and now that's being emphasized even more. I don't know what that's going to do to the company. The first thought is that it will make us look like other companies, but I don't think it will because we still have the spatial sense which I have not perceived in any other company, except in fits and starts. Other companies still don't conceive of space as a malleable, palpable material that you can mold as you will. That will always make us look different.

Murray is concerned of late with the whole dance profession; everyone in dance is beginning to look the same. As ballet dancers get modern technique and modern dancers get ballet technique everyone begins to look the same. So it's an evolving thing. I don't think we'll ever look like anyone else. Certainly, with our repertory we won't look like anyone else. But the look of the company is in flux. It's really fascinating to watch and as I get older I see these things, now.

Do you think Murray has changed his choreography?

Murray is proceeding along in a line. There haven't been any startling changes. *Index* [1973] was a startling departure from anything he'd done before, and *Porcelain* [1974] was a departure too. *Schubert,* which is fairly recent [1977] is directly related to *Proximities,* but is much more complex, refined, and sophisticated. I think he has been continuing along lines that have been going on in his head.

I don't think in terms of invention, structure, or craft that Murray's choreography has changed. It's in terms of what he wants out of his dancers that he has changed. Maybe this is because the company has changed, or maybe because he has changed as a performer. As he has been thinking about his own performance, his own choreography for himself has changed. His two new solo works, *Deja Vu* [1977] and *Suite for Erik* (which he choreographed for Erik Bruhn but now is going to do himself), have again enriched his thought about performing. It's amazing. He gets deeper and changes himself and it's wonderful to see. And he wants new things out of us too. It's challenging, and fascinating.

Murray's new group piece *Figura* is superficially different from anything that's gone before because he choreographed it specifically for the José Limón Company and for dancers from that technique.

We had a great deal to learn from working with them and they performed it in a certain way that Murray liked very much. He told us to begin to think of other ways to perform and to think about ourselves in other ways as performers, because we had got into what I call the *"Porcelain"* way of thinking–the nuance thing that we talked so much about. We had become used to that, and along comes the Limón company which has a dramatic heritage. The Limón company dances with a kind of passion, a nobility, which they got from José. On the other hand, we shy away from emotions.

Murray deliberately combined character and abstraction in *Figura.* He has told us that in our performance he wants us to have an idea of ourselves as characters dancing a role. That was a shocker for us because we have always worked with abstract principles. He said that we have that way of working down very well. Embodying the principles inherent in the choreography is taken as a matter of course, now we must get to a core of personality in the sense of a dramatic or narrative role.

It struck me that what he wants is what the old Nikolais-Louis dancers had—the strong central persona out of which the movement came. He now wants us to have the same feeling of a strong core of personality in this new piece and I think that's fascinating.

So what are you doing about Figura?

We were fortunate to have seen the Limón company perform it on stage and to see how they handled the idea of a character dancing the role. They went very far in that direction. They made characters for themselves out of those roles, and I had the feeling they were comfortable working that way because they have a very clear idea of how they feel about what they are dancing. As I said before, this is not something we are necessarily encouraged to show, and it went against the grain at first.

Right now we are rehearsing it and beginning to get our roles tailored to ourselves. I had the image in my mind of what Lane Sayles did with my role. I started out by actually copying one or two of his physical mannerisms, which were a lowered chin and a looking out from under the eyebrows. This seemed to me to be like a mask, very false and put on. As I do it I change it and it is changing into me rather than a copy of Lane. I really took only the idea of that strong visual image. We are extraordinarily different dancers and performers

and there is very little similarity between us. I put on this "mask" and
from there do the dance and try to keep the same attitude. In
rehearsal it will become clearer and clearer. Right now we can play
with it and rehearse it in different ways. Murray will be watching us
closely and what we are thinking about will come together with what
he wants.

*Your tours seem to be getting longer instead of shorter. A few years
ago you were saying that eleven weeks was just the edge of madness.
Last summer [78] you went on a twelve-week tour to Europe and in a
month you go on a sixteen-week tour to Europe. How do you feel
about that?*

Yes, our foreign tours are getting longer. Economics dictates it. I
must say however, that European tour was not so bad. In the middle
of the twelve weeks we had a week off. We could go anywhere we
wanted to and we didn't have a schedule. I went to the beach in
Spain and even though it rained, it was a nice change of scene.
　　During the last weeks, however, I began to get cabin fever in the
hotel rooms. Also, when I came back I had a period of adjustment to
get myself back together, but it's to be expected. When you return
you seem like such a stranger to friends and loved ones, but you learn
from past experience to expect that. I don't know about sixteen
weeks, but I guess I'll live.

I wanted to ask you about teaching now. Have you changed about that?

Well, for one thing I find I'm more amenable to teaching. I was
lukewarm about it several years ago. I don't think I would view
teaching as second-best now. I am at an age where I'm going to have
to think of what to do. I'm past thirty-six. I don't feel my performing
powers lessening, but it's time to think about it.
　　I think I could look forward to teaching. I have taught classes at
the school recently and I find that a teacher must be very grounded
in what he is teaching. A teacher must be able to see how the
students are working with the material or pulling away from the
material and know what to say to the students in order to bring them
back on the path. I find that I can see that much more easily now. I
find I can see the problem very directly in both technique and
improvisation classes. I've taught more, of course, and it all falls into
place—the material is beginning to organize itself.

What interests me is that I can see more. It has something to do with teaching. It has something to do with others trying to bring a clarity to themselves—students and younger dancers. I can see them struggling to make a clarity in their own performing and their own thinking and I think I can help them do that from my own experience. Also I can see where they are clear and where they are not clear. It has to do with the education of the eye—being able to spot what the difficulty is. That has suddenly become very interesting to me. Helping the younger dancers in the company work on things, suddenly something will hit me like a thunderclap and I'll make a suggestion and it works. Something clicks in their heads too, and that's very rewarding, and of course that's what the reward of the teacher is—to clarify something for someone else. The idea has entered their head and it belongs to them. They haven't just learned something out of a book. That's what a teacher does.

I suppose the teachers who made me excited did that for me. When you are young, you are so dumb you don't know these things. There are so many things that young people don't know, and they don't know they don't know, and so to help them is really wonderful. This is just a new thought to me, I've hardly expressed this even to myself. I'm trying to see if it has the idea of power or ego, though. Is this just some kind of power that I could have over people? This is a serious consideration. There are so many teachers who impose themselves on their students.

It interests me that you're thinking much more of teaching and remaining in dance.

Up until about one or two years ago I was stubbornly insistent that one did not have to stick with one area of endeavor and that one could change careers totally. One could go off and do radio electronics or something, as a defiance of fate, a defiance of karma. But I see now that the idea of karma, to put it very crudely, is that you make your own bed and then you have to lie in it. What you work at all those years makes a dent in the world around you and also you're forming your own self to it. You don't need to break out and do something completely different in order to progress or to find out about life and living. You become wise and it's a pity to waste the experience. Although I hate the idea that you might become a teacher for that reason—in order not to waste the experience. I would rather

play around with radio tubes than become a teacher for the wrong
reasons.

Do you feel that your own dancing has changed?

Yes. Certainly since we last spoke. I have a new freedom in my back.
That era of problems is gone. It's changed my dancing—my back and
spine are much looser.

I don't work at dancing as hard as I used to. I don't have to
push so hard in order to accomplish the same ends on stage.
Economy. I guess as you get older you don't have to squander yourself
so much. It's not that you get tired, it fits into a definition of grace,
i.e., what the movement requires without overdoing it or underdoing
it. Graceful movement is just the right amount of energy for what
you're doing. It's not smoothing out everything or making everything
look pretty—it's using just the right amount.

I can do that more. I can feel in my bones earlier when
rehearsing a piece, what is required. I don't need to do it in front of
an audience in order to find out what's required in terms of letting
out or pulling back, in terms of the right amount of energy. I intuit it
sooner and consequently I wear myself out less, and I think my
command on stage is greater. I think it's more compelling to look at.
It makes dancing less frustrating and a lot more fun. Less exhausting,
more satisfying. It's nice.

*Have you been working on this? What have you been doing that made
this happen?*

I went through a lot of performances delivering at a level. On a long
tour it can become rote and the way you go into it is always the same
and it doesn't make you grow. It's not interesting, it's not satisfying.
So in the last year I have been really concentrating in rehearsal time.
I've been doing everything at performance pitch. We talked about
this before, but I've been concentrating on this much more and can
see how important it is. I really dislike running through anything at
less than performance pitch. I've found marking through pieces or
being off-and-on in pieces—marking sections that I knew were okay
and then putting on more energy, or thundering into things that I
thought needed work—was exhausting. It didn't work because my
energy level was going up and down all the time and it became
irritating. So now I do everything at performance pitch because it's

less exhausting and I learn more about what I'm doing. Also what other people are doing around me seems to count more. I am more receptive at that pitch than the off-and-on kind of pitch. When you are off-and-on you become quite self-involved, whereas performance pitch requires that you be open to all the things coming in around you, and that will change you even without your thinking about it.

I rarely get physically exhausted anymore, and I used to—especially when my back was so bad. That was an energy blockage and when the energy doesn't flow you get tired. When it *does* flow you can just float along on it and it's wonderful. It's a miracle.

How did your back problem contribute to the way you changed?

Working through it and forcing me to say to myself—why? Why do I have this knot of tension in my middle? Why is the energy stopping there? It can be partly just the way you are living, it can be partly emotional problems, but if you know how to work physically in a certain way, without stopping yourself, the flow goes into all parts of your life and you don't make problems for yourself. Consequently your physical organism is much more at ease with itself, and mine certainly is now. I still have unexplained tensions but I've become sensitive to their presence. I would like to direct my life so that I don't have these stoppages. I'm not sure these tensions always yield to examination but still, I would like to know about them. I've just started to take up yoga and that has helped enormously.

There is so much hard work for a dancer. I sometimes look at the younger ones and wonder what is sustaining them.

The whole scene has changed drastically because money has come in. It was not there before. There's a possibility for a career now. The interest was always there but the idea of making a living at it was not. Now you can make a living. You can come to New York, but now there are also jobs around the country in regional companies. You can live in Pittsburgh and make a living as a dancer, in Salt Lake City, Minneapolis—almost anywhere. That would have been impossible five years ago. In a sense, this fans the interest—it makes the competition keener.

What do you say today about coming to New York?

Actually you can come to New York at any age. It helps if you have

maturity. It helps if you have money. No, you have to have maturity.
You can be any age but you have to have a certain amount of
perspective about life because life will drown you in this city if you
don't watch out. There is too much to do, too much to see, too many
kinds of people, and there is too high an energy level to go into it
unprepared, undefensive.

I think if I had come to New York any sooner than I did, which
was at the age of twenty-three, I would have been pulled apart by the
ferocious energies of the city. That sounds pretty abstract, but once
you get here you know what I'm talking about. The vibration in the
air is enough to set your nerves a-tingle. It isn't just danger from
muggers, and it isn't just traffic, and it isn't just smog or buildings or
whatever. It's a way of life. It's a more intense living energy, and if
you come from the placid Midwest or the relaxed West Coast you're
not prepared to hold all that off and concentrate on your study, which
is what you have to do. I would say to any dance student, don't come
to New York City unless you know what you are going to study and
with whom. And don't come with less than eight hundred dollars or a
lot of friends who can take care of you, because the living situation
can be a terrible hassle.

I've noticed students at concerts recently. They have a nervous
look on their faces; they're struggling through their student days in
the city until they can get a job. But the thing that sustains them
seems to be getting the job rather than becoming a dancer, because
technically they are already as good as any of the professional dancers
of ten years ago. The technical level is so good now that the
competition is very keen. There are more jobs but you still have to be
in the right place at the right time. Everyone is under a great strain,
waiting, hoping, and wishing. It seems like a ghastly, nervous burden
to put on them but, in a sense, you get better dancers in the
companies.

But what is sustaining them?

I really think it is glory. I really think it's the chance to be on the
stage and be another Judith Jamison or a Baryshnikov.

*Something has to draw people on. Think of all the physical work that
goes into it.*

Young people are less afraid of physical hard work than they used to be. Of course there is a big upsurge in keeping fit, which is healthy. People are less apt to expect that they can get through life without physical exertion. Science has found that an active physical life promotes health, promotes longevity, and so young people expect to do that more. Physical athletic programs are booming, amateur dance programs are booming as exercise, for health. People are less afraid to go into dance and once they do, they find out how much fun it is. And it *is* fun at first, until you get serious, then it starts to hurt. When I was young the work itself was fun to do and that draws you on and the encouragement of teachers draws you on until the pain becomes really intense, and then something else has to lead you on.

What makes that final push between being a professional student and being a professional dancer?

You dance along for a number of years. There's that awful point between when you end being a student and when you begin being a professional. It isn't necessarily when you have the job with the company. Everyone senses it, I think, in their own development, even if they don't admit it to themselves, that they have come to the end of their student days. If they have the prospect of a job, or if they start their own company or have some way of going on to the next step, then they'll keep going to classes. If they think physically they just cannot go any further, if they are discouraged, if they think that there is no opportunity—well, everyone has to come to terms with what they have to give, with what the opportunities are and it's very hard.

For me it was not hard—everything just slid into place. And in that sense there are a number of questions I never had to face. But in my case I've had Murray Louis around and he is an incredibly strong person, a strong spirit. He's a whole way of life—he's a force of nature, take it or leave it. If you can't accept that about him you can leave him and go off. I stuck around him through all my self-questionings because regardless of what you may like or may not like about the man, you cannot question him as an artist. He is what he is and that is so admirable. He's difficult to live with, but I have boundless admiration for him. Some people cannot take that intensity. It has hit me in various ways. But life is a little easier now. He's changed and I've changed. That's life.

Appendix:
Choreography by Murray Louis

*Works by Murray Louis mentioned in the text
in order of composition*

Suite

Performed by:	Murray Louis, Gladys Bailin, Coral Martindale, Beverly Schmidt
Music:	Johann Sebastian Bach (Brandenburg Concerto No. 2 and Gavotte from Orchestral Suite No. 1).
Costumes:	Ruth Taube
Premiere:	November 17, 1956 Henry Street Playhouse New York City

Calligraph for Martyrs*

Performed by:	Murray Louis, Bill Frank, Albert Reid
Music:	Alwin Nikolais
Design:	John Hultberg
Costumes:	Frank Garcia
Premiere:	November 24, 1961 Henry Street Playhouse New York City

---

Calligraph for Martyrs was called *Signal* for its first performance. It was first performed with its present title on December 7, 1962 and was designed by Alwin Nikolais under the pseudonym, Nick Loper.

Facets

Performed by:	Murray Louis, Gladys Bailin
Music:	Alwin Nikolais
Costumes:	Frank Garcia
Premiere:	November 23, 1962
	Henry Street Playhouse
	New York City

Interims

Performed by:	Murray Louis, Phyllis Lamhut, Bill Frank, Roger Rowell
Music:	Lukas Foss *(Timecycle)*
Lighting and scenic design:	Nick Loper*
Costumes:	Frank Garcia
Premiere:	November 29, 1963
	Henry Street Playhouse
	New York City

Landscapes

Performed by:	Murray Louis and Susan Buirge, Ann Carlton, Mimi Garrard, Janet Strader, Wanda Pruska, Meikle Guy— understudy
Music:	Alvin Walker
Design:	Nick Loper*
Costumes:	Frank Garcia
Premiere:	November 20, 1964
	Henry Street Playhouse
	New York City

*Pseudonym for Alwin Nikolais

Junk Dances

Performed by:	Murray Louis, Phyllis Lamhut and Susan Buirge, Ann Carlton, Mimi Garrard, Janet Strader
Music:	Arranged
Design:	Robert Wilson (1964) Murray Stern (1966)
Premiere:	November 27, 1964 Henry Street Playhouse New York City

Chimera*

Performed by:	Murray Louis
Music:	Alwin Nikolais
Setting and costumes:	Margo Hoff
Premiere:	February 25, 1966 Henry Street Playhouse New York City

Concerto

Performed by:	Murray Louis
Music:	Johann Sebastian Bach (Concerto No. 1 for Harpsichord—piano used)
Design:	Paul von Ringelhein
Costumes:	Frank Garcia
Premiere:	December 15, 1966 Henry Street Playhouse New York City

Go 6**

Performed by:	Murray Louis, Carolyn Carlson, Phyllis Lamhut, Wanda Pruska, Michael Ballard, Bill Frank, Raymond Johnson
Music:	Arnold Heinrich***
Costumes:	Frank Garcia

*Called *Charade* until October, 1966
**Called *Go 7* in first performances
***Pseudonym for Alwin Nikolais

Premiere:	October 1, 1967 East St. Louis Illinois
New York premiere:	February 6, 1969 Henry Street Playhouse New York City

Proximities

Performed by:	Murray Louis, Michael Ballard, Raymond Johnson, Phyllis Lamhut, Sara Shelton, Frances Tabor
Music:	Johannes Brahms (Serenade in A—1st, 2nd, 4th, and 5th movements)
Lighting:	Alwin Nikolais
Costumes:	Frank Garcia
Premiere:	January 30, 1969 Henry Street Playhouse New York City

Intersection

Performed by:	Murray Louis, Michael Ballard, Raymond Johnson, Sara Shelton, Frances Tabor
Music:	Harold Faberman
Background projections:	David Preston
Costumes:	Frank Garcia and Lynn Levine
Premiere:	February 13, 1969 Henry Street Playhouse New York City

Personnae

Performed by:	Murray Louis, Michael Ballard, Raymond Johnson, Sara Shelton

Music:	Free Life Communication
Lighting:	Alwin Nikolais
Costumes:	Frank Garcia
Premiere:	January 5, 1971 Chicago Civic Theater Chicago, Illinois
New York premiere:	January 19, 1972 Brooklyn Academy of Music Brooklyn, N.Y.

Continuum

Performed by:	Murray Louis, Michael Ballard, Les Ditson, Raymond Johnson, Helen Kent, Sara Shelton, Marcia Wardell
Music:	Corky Siegel Blues Band; Alwin Nikolais
Lighting:	Alwin Nikolais
Costumes:	Frank Garcia
Premiere:	January 5, 1971 Chicago Civic Theater Chicago, Illinois
New York premiere:	January 20, 1972 Brooklyn Academy of Music Brooklyn, N.Y.

Disguise

Performed by:	Murray Louis, Michael Ballard, Les Ditson, Raymond Johnson, Helen Kent, Sara Shelton
Music:	Arranged by Corky Siegel and Alwin Nikolais
Costumes:	Malcolm McCormick

NOTE: *Personnae, Continuum* and *Disguise* were performed together under the collective title *A.D. Opus XLIV.*

Premiere:	January 5, 1971 Chicago Civic Theater Chicago, Illinois (Dropped from repertory)

Hoopla

Performed by:	Murray Louis, Michael Ballard, Les Ditson, Anne McLeod (Ditson), Helen Kent, Robert Small, Marcia Wardell
Music:	Lisbon State Police Band; sound effects
Lighting:	Alwin Nikolais
Costumes:	Frank Garcia
Premiere:	January 26, 1972 Brooklyn Academy of Music Brooklyn, New York

Cast

Opening:	The Company
Solo:	Murray Louis
Ringmaster:	Michael Ballard, Anne McLeod, Marcia Wardell
The Three-headed worm:	Les Ditson, Helen Kent, Robert Small
Duet:	Murray Louis, Michael Ballard
Magic act:	Les Ditson, Helen Kent, Anne McLeod, Robert Small, Marcia Wardell
The Flower:	Murray Louis, Michael Ballard
Balancing act (The Gold trio):	Marcia Wardell, Les Ditson, Robert Small
Silver man:	Murray Louis
Bows:	The Company

Index (to necessary neuroses . . .)

Performed by:	Murray Louis, Michael Ballard, Les Ditson, Helen Kent, Anne McLeod, Robert Small, Marcia Wardell
Music:	Oregon Ensemble
Lighting:	Alwin Nikolais
Costumes:	Frank Garcia
Premiere:	February 15, 1973 Brooklyn Academy of Music Brooklyn, N.Y.

Porcelain Dialogues

Performed by:	Michael Ballard, Richard Haisma, Helen Kent, Anne McLeod, Robert Small, Marcia Wardell
Music:	P.I. Tchaikovsky (Quartet in D Major —1st and 2nd movements and a reprise of 1st movement)
Lighting:	Alwin Nikolais
Costumes:	Frank Garcia
Premiere:	February 19, 1974 Lyceum Theatre New York City

Scheherazade

Performed by:	Murray Louis, Michael Ballard, Richard Haisma, Helen Kent, Anne McLeod, Robert Small, Marcia Wardell

Music:	Nikolai Rimsky-Korsakov, Alwin Nikolais, Free life Communication. Rimsky-Korsakov themes arranged and adapted by Jeff Kent, Doug Lubahn, and George Wadenius
Still Photography:	Tom Caravaglia
Lighting:	Alwin Nikolais
Costumes:	Frank Garcia
Premiere: (In two acts)	January 18, 1974 Clowes Memorial Hall Indianapolis, Indiana
New York premiere:	February 21, 1974 Lyceum Theatre New York City
Premiere (In three acts)	November 9, 1974 Wisconsin Union Theater Madison, Wisconsin
New York premiere:	December 27, 1974 New York University Theatre New York City

Cast

The Dreamer:	Murray Louis
Scheherazade:	Michael Ballard
Their dreams:	Richard Haisma, Helen Kent, Anne McLeod, Robert Small, Marcia Wardell

Geometrics

Performed by:	Michael Ballard, Richard Haisma, Helen Kent, Anne McLeod, Jerry Pearson, Sara Pearson, Robert Small, Marcia Wardell
Music:	Alwin Nikolais
Lighting:	Alwin Nikolais
Costumes:	Frank Garcia

Premiere:	December 20, 1974 New York University Theatre New York City

*Moment**

Performed by:	Rudolf Nureyev with Brian Burn, Roy Campbell-Moore, Gavin Dorrian, and Richard Holland of The Scottish Ballet
Music:	Maurice Ravel (Quartet in F)
Costumes:	Frank Garcia**
Lighting:	Alwin Nikolais**
Premiere:	September 19, 1975 Teatro Zarzuela Madrid, Spain
New York premiere:	Rudolf Nureyev with Michael Ballard, Richard Haisma, Jerry Pearson, Robert Small November 18, 1975 Uris Theatre New York City
Company premiere:	Murray Louis with Michael Ballard, Richard Haisma, Jerry Pearson, Robert Small December 19, 1975 New York University Theatre New York City

Catalogue

Performed by:	Michael Ballard, Richard Haisma, Helen Kent, Dianne Markham, Anne McLeod, Jerry Pearson, Sara Pearson, Robert Small
Music:	Victor Herbert

*Name later changed to *Moments*
*Listed as Barrow in first programs

Lighting:	Alwin Nikolais
Costumes:	Judith Graese (executed by Frank Garcia)
Slides:	Tom Caravaglia, Mark Jacobs
Premiere:	December 19, 1975 New York University Theatre New York City

Cast

The men and the women:	Michael Ballard, Richard Haisma, Helen Kent, Dianne Markham, Anne McLeod, Jerry Pearson, Robert Small
America's sweetheart:	Sara Pearson, Michael Ballard, Richard Haisma, Jerry Pearson, Robert Small
First woman:	Anne McLeod
At the beach:	Helen Kent, Michael Ballard, Dianne Markham, Richard Haisma
Second woman:	Sara Pearson
Beautiful island:	Anne McLeod, Richard Haisma
Coquette:	Helen Kent, Michael Ballard
Third woman:	Dianne Markham
High society:	Anne McLeod, Robert Small, Sara Pearson, Jerry Pearson
Fourth woman:	Helen Kent
Reprise:	The Men
The March:	The Women

Glances

Performed by:	Michael Ballard, Richard Haisma, Helen Kent, Anne McLeod, Dianne

	Markham, Jerry Pearson, Sara Pearson, Robert Small
Music:	Dave Brubeck (arranged by Darius Brubeck)
Costumes:	Frank Garcia
Premiere:	August 6, 1976 Palmer Auditorium Connecticut College New London, Connecticut
New York premiere:	February 10, 1977 Beacon Theater New York City

Deja Vu

Performed by:	Murray Louis
Music:	Tarrega, Lauro, Scarlatti, and Albeniz
Lighting:	Alwin Nikolais
Costumes:	Frank Garcia
Premiere:	February 16, 1977 Beacon Theater New York City

Schubert

Performed by:	Michael Ballard, Janis Brenner, William Holahan, Dianne Markham, Anne McLeod, Jerry Pearson, Sara Pearson, Robert Small
Music:	Franz Schubert (Quintet in A Major, "Trout"—1st, 2nd, and 4th movements.)
Lighting Design:	Alwin Nikolais
Costumes:	Frank Garcia
Premiere:	October 14, 1977 Lisner Auditorium Washington, D.C.

New York premiere:	March 9, 1978 Brooklyn Academy of Music Brooklyn, New York

Figura

Performed by:	Carla Maxwell, Lane Sayles, Douglas Varone, Nina Watt of the José Limon Company
Music:	Paul Winter Consort; Lecuona; Segovia.
Lighting Design:	Richard Nelson
Costumes:	Frank Garcia
Premiere: (Limon Company)	November 6, 1978 Popejoy Hall University of New Mexico Albuquerque, New Mexico
New York premiere: (Limon Company)	December 19, 1978 New York City Center New York City
Premiere: (Louis Company)	October 9, 1979 Eisenhower Auditorium State College, Pennsylvania
Performed by:	Michael Ballard, Anne McLeod, Sara Pearson, William Holahan
New York premiere: (Louis Company)	November 2, 1979 New York City Center New York City
Performed by:	Michael Ballard, Anne McLeod, Sara Pearson, William Holahan

*Five Haikus**

Performed by:	Murray Louis
Music:	Alexander Scriabin (Piano Préludes)
Costumes:	Frank Garcia
Premiere:	April 11, 1979
	Centre Georges Pompidou
	Paris, France
New York Premiere:	November 2, 1979
	New York City Center
	New York City

*Called *Suite for Erik* in first performances.